04/2013 - LOCAL AUTHOR

Embracing Beauty

*Practical Style for
Every Shape and Season
of Motherhood*

Trina Holden

Visit http://trinaholden.com to purchase additional copies. Thank you.

Edited by Jennifer Lambert (http://jenniferalambert.com) and Gretchen Acheson (http://gretchenlouise.com).

Layout and design by Jeremy Holden.

All Scripture quotations are from the English Standard Version unless otherwise noted.

This book contains affiliate links.

ISBN - 978-1483917672

Dedication

for Mom, of course
and for my babes:
Jesse, Claire, Seth, and #4
it's a joy to find the beauty in each day with you

Contents

Forward

I'm probably the least qualified person to write a forward to a book about fashion. I've felt unfashionable my entire life. I've had a tug-of-war with my identity as a woman ever since my mom died a week to the day after my 18th birthday. I grew up with brothers and I have two sons. Even the kids I sponsor through Compassion International are both boys. I'm not the girly-girl. And then God gave me a daughter. And my world as I knew it broke into a hundred tiny pieces of what I thought I knew about beauty and was put back together by this child. This child, I want to grow up into a deeply rooted sense of her own beauty as a creature made in God's image. I never want the mirror to be the boss of her. I want her to have a glorious security in her body and to know that it's never what she puts on the outside but always what takes place on the inside that will make her beautiful.

But I know she will only learn by seeing what I do. So I must make peace with myself and my womanhood as well as my closet. And in the midst of this journey I've discovered a sense of humor and a community of women, like Trina, who love me just the way I am. Some days in sweat pants and week old mascara. Some days in a new top and pair of jeans I'm breaking in. I've learned that when I feel beautiful on the inside my outsides usually match up. That friends willing to share their coats are priceless and that at the end of the day my husband always prefers me best when fresh-faced and wearing an old T-shirt before bed.

So I dance with Zoe around our bedroom and we try on clothes together and laugh at our goofy reflections in the mirror. Her dad sweeps her off her feet and we pray beauty into the core of her being, cemented away in her heart before the world can start to offer her another message. We pray she doesn't just know she is beloved just the way she is, but that she actually believes it. No matter what she's wearing. So that she's free to enjoy clothes rather than be intimidated by them. So that she feels just as comfortable in a pair of sweat pants as she does dressed up for a wedding. That she is the most at home in her own skin and that "beautiful, beloved, redeemed" are the only labels she cares about.

"He has made everything beautiful in its time." Ecclesiastes 3:11

That includes you and me and our daughters. May we embrace our womanhood and delight in the fun of finding beauty in a hundred different places. I'm so grateful to Trina for a book that helps guide us in that search. To uncover the joy in the journey of getting dressed. To replacein dread with expectation, isolation with community, and fashion with a way of seeing differently. Seeing ourselves through the eyes of our Creator who rejoices over us no matter what we're wearing.

Here's to sweat pant days and dressed up high heels celebrations. Here's to the glory of the ordinary and the wonder of a body that can birth babies. Here's to that sweater your kids colored all over and those boots your daughter loves to dress up in. Here's to women who see themselves always reflected first in the eyes of a loving Father and give themselves and their waistlines grace. No matter what the mirror tells you, I assure you that you are more beautiful today than you were three kids ago.

Yours with love, laughter and usually unblow-dried hair,

Lisa-Jo Baker

Author of the upcoming book, "Surprised by Motherhood:
Everything I never expected about being a mom"
(Tyndale House, Spring 2014)

Blogger at lisajobaker.com

Introduction

The Journey to Embracing Beauty

My journey to finding my style as a mamma has had more twists and turns than the average murder mystery.

I could claim I had a head start, being born to a mother who has impeccable taste and perennial style. She has never succumbed to fads, but has always looked stylish no matter what season of life she is in. I remember watching with fascination as my mother French braided her hair on Sunday mornings, and I noticed even at a young age that my mom didn't dress like everyone else's mom. She had her own style and she always looked amazing. It was a promising beginning.

But then my life took a style-defining twist. Just before my 13th birthday, when I was finally starting to notice trends and wonder what my own personal style might be—my family moved to a primitive homestead in rural, upstate NY. We lived in a tipi for 7 months while we built a log cabin, and our style took a dive. Not only was my wardrobe shrunk to whatever fit in a cardboard box under my cot, but at the same time we had aligned ourselves with a subset of the Christian community that held to very conservative clothing standards. Earrings, bright colors, and anything but ankle length skirts were tabooed. The sole purpose of a woman's attire was to cover her body, neck to toes, and by all means, let nothing attract attention.

The Lean Years

For a few years there, it was a style desert. Mom and I wore denim skirts and jumpers with shirts in dark, neutral shades. Hair was a thing to be pulled out of the way of the work that needed to be done. Accessories beyond layers that kept frost bite at bay were non-existent.

Gradually my parents came to the conclusion that fabrics other than denim were not inherently evil, and that a little beauty and individuality might be good for morale. It was a turning point when Mom put her earrings back in, and got her scarf basket out of storage. Once again I enjoyed watching my mom's style come out, despite living in the boonies and only affording half-off day at the local thrift store.

But me? I was too busy gardening, learning to cook, and running my little home business to put much effort into defining my style. I went to my mom and sisters for advice, and usually wore whatever they nodded "yes" to. Most days I didn't even know how frumpy I looked 'cause I didn't have much to compare myself to (remember, we lived in the boonies and had no TV), and even more often, I couldn't have cared less. I'd spent too many years under teachings that equated individual style with immodesty, and I had decided to play it safe and stick with classic lines, blah colors, with hardly a trace of anything artistic or personal. I'd fully adopted the mistaken belief that clothing was a means to achieving purity, rather than a canvas on which to express the beauty God put inside each of us.

By the time we left the homestead in my early twenties, we'd nearly completed the transition out of our more legalistic dressing standards, but I still wasn't spending hours in front of the mirror crafting my personal style statement. What effort I did extend was in the area of my newest interest—vintage costume. I could put together a French Revolution era ensemble that could knock your stockings off, but when tasked at coming up with a modern day outfit, I struggled to get pants to meet my ankles and shirts to fit my 5'9" frame, much less come up with an outfit that was a confident expression of my personal taste.

The Plot Thickens

Then I entered motherhood—that blessed season when you are never the same size three weeks in a row. As I struggled to reacquaint myself with my own body, another subconscious factor was working against any progress I could make in defining my style.

Since I was a young child, I had lived under the mistaken impression that my worth was largely based on people's good opinion of me. This was crippling to any effort to be myself when I dressed because I lived in terror of accruing someone's negative opinion of any aspect of my outfit. When my first child was 5 months old, my anxiety reached a peak that actually landed me in the ER with severe chest pain. After discerning that my physical distress was actually due to the mental strain I was under to please everyone and their next door neighbor, I was given the opportunity to view every area of my life, including what I wore, from a renewed perspective.

A Turning Point

That year marked a turning point in my life in so many ways. The Lord actually quite swiftly delivered me from what was a severe anxiety disorder (I share that journey in this series of posts on my blog) and I began to taste what it was like to live free. This freedom extended to my wardrobe, although I was still quite misled on what made a good outfit.

With three pregnancies in five years and little time for shopping, my closet was filled with a collection of jeans that spanned 6 sizes but little else that fit, much less flattered. Too often I still made outfit decisions based more on practicality than personality. *"This doesn't have spit-up on it—score!"*

I knew how to thrift shop, sew for myself, and style my hair, but even when I had energy to invest in my appearance, I was still lost. I often chose an item just because it actually fit, or because it was really cheap, or because it was what I thought was my favorite color, but rarely all three. With a closet full of clothes, I still spent many Sunday mornings crying pitifully in my bedroom at a loss as to what to wear to church.

And this is where, if this were a murder mystery, someone would probably commit suicide by hanging themselves in a closet with an old belt. Except that's not what happened. This is actually where the story takes a graceful turn and a giant leap forward. This is when all my experiences up to that point converged with some timely advice and the example of some other moms who were really rocking their personal style, and I finally learned to feel cute and fashionable despite my waist's six year identity crisis.

This is where my story intersects yours and we learn together how to rock our mamma style.

Where are you in your fashion journey? Do you struggle to justify the time spent on dressing yourself when there's a minivan full of kids who still need you to tie their shoes? Are you lost when it comes to knowing what makes you feel cute or glamorous? Are time and money the biggest barriers between you and a great wardrobe?

Girlfriend—there's hope! Let's learn together how to embrace beauty in this season!

{While I was writing this book, I had many conversations with women whom I had observed embracing beauty in their daily lives, and we talked about what motivated them. I was amazed, once I opened up the subject, how much passion and joy some of these women were experiencing. I will be sharing some of their thoughts and stories throughout the book to help give a fuller picture of what the journey to embracing beauty can look like.}

Expressing God's Glory
{Making the Case for Beauty}

You can tell from my journey that I have had some serious issues about getting dressed. Mine had to do with worrying I wouldn't meet someone else's modesty standards, or using a standard of dress to define purity. These issues may be foreign to you, but trust me, *we all have issues.*

The point of this chapter is to help us move beyond all our issues and determine what the real purpose of outward adornment is. We need to discern a solid "why" because the reality is, no matter how many books you read, how many Pinterest boards you scan, or how many episodes of "What Not to Wear" you ingest, if you don't have the proper motivation, you'll not follow through to successfully embracing beauty in the season of motherhood.

- Why, when dishes and laundry and another dirty diaper comes flying at you, would you even bother to get out of your P.J.'s?

- Why, when you never go anywhere but the grocery store, should you learn to accessorize?

- Why, when your clothes *never* fit, is it still worth it to get out of your yoga pants and try to look put-together?

So often, we are motivated, but with the wrong "why". Let's look at a few of the common motivations for getting dressed up, and how they eventually fail us…

Dressing for "Them"

For years, I dressed with the goal to conform and to please "them"—those unnamed hoards I imagined looking on me in judgment. Was she modest enough? Classy enough? Did her clothes fit her figure? Did she even know how to match? This is a very strong motivator, and got me through my entire teens. The problem with this motivation is that it is a form of bondage… the bondage of living to please other people. It is based on the lie that our worth comes from what other people think of us. When the Lord finally delivered me from this lie, my motivation dried up! I can remember thinking, "Why should I even bother to dress up?"

Dressing for Friends

'Fess up… this is a huge motivation, isn't it? We dress up so we can meet our friends' approval, and hopefully even get a "wow" out of them, right? I think we can all see, though it hurts to admit it, that this motivation comes from pride. We dress up in order to build ourselves up in other's eyes. Again, this motivation falls flat when we embrace the truth that our worth comes from God and the dwelling of His Spirit within us.

Clearly, these motivations aren't adequate. We need to get to a deeper why—we need to ask: why did God create beauty, and what should our response be?

When I first began this book, I had some great ideas for the "how" of dressing our ever-changing mommy bodies, but I soon realized I really had a very vague idea of what God's purpose might be in our adornment.

So, I went to the scriptures to see what God said about beauty. Thus began a journey I will not soon forget—the journey of discovering God's heart for beauty. What I share with you in this chapter will, I'm sure, not do the subject justice, but I've found that trying to write about beauty is like trying to put a rainbow in a bottle. There are so many facets to beauty and why we, as children of God, are called to embrace it, I can only hope to reveal, as it were, a portion of this gift.

It is my hope as we dwell on several of God's purposes in our beauty, that you will find one or two that resonate with you, and give you the motivation you need to continue the journey.

Embracing Beauty as an Act of Worship

"From Zion, perfect in beauty, God shines forth."
Psalm 50:2 NIV

God is where beauty began. Not only did He create beauty, it's an element of His very being. Beautiful is something God can't not be, and beauty is something He can't not create. He created us in His image, as both a reflection of His beauty, and a celebration of His love for beautiful things. To Him you are His crowning achievement in a world full of beauty. (Meditate on that next time you're having a bad hair day!)

Because beauty is an attribute of God and something He is passionate about, anything we do to recognize and embrace beauty can actually become an act of worship. Pausing to take in a sunset, admiring the delicate beauty of a flower, and agreeing with Him as to the beauty of the body He gave us, honors His design and skill as creator, and this is worship.

Embracing Beauty as a Reflection of God's Character

It's not only in accepting the design of our bodies that honors God, but the entire process of embracing beauty can reflect, or give a picture of, our God to those around us. Throughout scripture and creation, we see a beautiful God, celebrating beauty in every place, in every moment, and in every creature He created. When we embrace this same passion for beauty and creativity, we give a picture of His character to the world around us. He made us each incredibly unique, and creating pleasing outfits that speak of our individuality can shine a light on His vast imagination and power as Creator.

My sister Anja went through a season of questioning the validity of pursuing beauty—here's what God whispered to her heart…

"A few years ago I became concerned that my obsession with beauty and fashion was an idol in my life. I thought of going on a fashion fast: wearing only plain old jeans and a plain old t-shirt. The very thought almost sent me into spasms. But then the Lord showed me that my love for beauty and to be beautiful comes directly from the heart of the Father because I was created in His image.

"I struggled in the past with the fact that I was not a musician and I was envious that musicians get to worship God with their work all the time. But what God has showed me was that when I take delight in the beauty that He created and when I create a masterpiece—whether it is an actual piece of artwork, an outfit that makes me feel beautiful, or adding a garnish to each plate of desert before it leaves the kitchen—that those acts of creating beauty are a form of worship.

"We are not all created the same, for some of us it is not the beauty of paint splattered on canvas that makes our soul sing but instead it is crunching of numbers and solving of math problems, or maybe it is writing, planting a garden, or grafting an apple tree. We are created to worship God with the gifting that He has given us and just because I can't play the guitar does not mean my

worship to Him is any less sweet. God created me with a little extra helping of the love of beauty and when I look up in delight to see what shape the clouds are in today it puts a great big smile on my Father's face. And when I choose to create something beautiful it sends a sweet-smelling incense of worship to the throne room."

Embracing Beauty as a Witness to Others

I used to wear a lot of neutrals and "quiet" colors. My outfits rarely made a statement, but rather did a good job of helping me fade into the background. Looking back I realize this was because of the fear in my life. Since the Lord set me free from my anxiety disorder, I have tended toward brighter colors and not-so-quiet style statements. This boldness stems from the joy I feel in the freedom Christ has given me. I have even been known to wear wigs or period costumes to events that are not costume parties, simply because I love to dress up, and I continue to revel in the freedom He's given me to not worry what other people think about me.

What do your clothes say about you? Do they declare that you are redeemed? I'm not talking about an "I love Jesus" T-shirt. I'm talking about walking fully in the freedom and beauty He designed us for. When we embrace our personal style, free from the bondage of insecurities and fear, people will see a difference. They will be drawn to the layers of grace and joy that you wear, allowing you to share in a winsome way what God has done in your life.

Embracing Beauty as an Element of Self-Care

Because beauty is an element of God's character, and He created us in His image, there's no question that cultivating that area of our lives is rejuvenating to us on many levels. Order and beauty in my home inspire and delight me. Making an effort toward style and order in my personal appearance does the same.

My friend, Amanda[1], sees beauty as a crucial part of being the mom God has called her to be…

"I like to think of beauty as being the natural result of self-care. Our bodies are God's creation, and the Bible even says that our bodies are His temple (1 Cor. 6:19). So to me, self-care and beauty are a matter of stewardship of His gift to us. Personally, my outside is a direct reflection of what is going on inside. When I am not taking care of my physical body through proper rest, diet, and exercise, you will often find me slacking in how I care for my skin, hair, and how I dress. Beauty is important to me because it is the evidence that I am taking care of my body, His temple.

"When I am taking care of myself on the inside and out, I am a much happier mom. I am more motivated, more creative, and more intentional. So instead of seeing self-care and beauty as something I am too busy for, I see it as a necessary step to being the mother I want to be."

Do you ever feel guilty taking time to care for yourself? You shouldn't. Taking care of our bodies is a way we ready ourselves to serve with the joy God desires His children to walk in.

Embracing Beauty as a Gift to Others

I've heard it said that "being well dressed is a beautiful form of politeness." Our outward appearance does significantly affect those around us, so it is not wrong to think of others in our pursuit of beauty. But it should stem from a place of confidence in our worth before God, not from insecurities. It should be with the intent to bless the people who have to look at us, not simply to impress them. Our pursuit of beauty should flow out of a desire to embrace more fully the woman God says we are, not just another attempt to meet someone's expectation of us. He has called you beautiful, sister—don't dilute that calling to a list of ought's and should's.

A Gift to our Husbands

I think that adorning ourselves for our men (whether in the bedroom or out and about) is just like putting icing on a cake. Cake without icing is still good—it's cake, people! But add the icing and you've got something special. We can bless our men by stepping out of the ordinary and adding a layer of sweet to the woman God put in His life.

It's a man's nature to be visually attracted to us, but often we take their love and commitment for granted and slack off in our attempts to romance them visually. My friend, Ginger[2], has a great story about loving her man in the busy season of little ones…

> *"When I was in my early 20's, and my first two babies were two years old and four months old, I decided I would stop wearing makeup. At first hubby was okay with it. But one day, he and the kids were waiting in the car for me. When I got in he said, 'The kids and I decided we really like it more when you wear makeup.' I had to laugh, because obviously the kids were too little for an opinion, but I was so glad he told me he preferred makeup! Over the 21 years of our marriage I have always been able to count on him to be 100% honest when I ask about my appearance. I think this is because early in our marriage I received his remark about the makeup without getting upset or going on about how hard it is to get ready in the morning with two little ones, etc. Our appearance is important to our husbands, but I don't think they are always comfortable saying so because they don't want to appear shallow or critical."*

A Gift to our Children

As mothers, we are the first to define beauty for our daughters and our sons. Is the way we dress telling them that God makes everything beautiful, or that beauty is an optional part of life? If Mommy, with extra weight or tired lines, can still dress tastefully and smile at her day and her children, they will see that beauty is not confined to the cover of a shiny magazine, but that they live with a beautiful woman every day.

Fresh Motivation

And so we see that God's purpose in our beauty is that we would embrace it as an aspect of His character that He planted in us. In doing so, we will experience joy, draw others to Himself, and bring Him glory.

But how do we do this? How do we practically embrace beauty and reflect His glory today, with this body, that clothing budget, and those few precious moments a mother can call her own?

First of all, by accepting the shape you're in now. By believing Him when He says you are beautiful, and dressing well for your current body type, instead of being in denial or trying to hide your body in layers of frumpy clothes. We'll discuss that in the next chapter.

With all this focus on personal appearance, it will be important that we maintain balance and a Biblical perspective on beauty, so we'll talk about that in Chapter 3.

Once we accept the truth that He's made us each uniquely beautiful, and have a balanced idea of pursuing beauty, then we'll be ready to dive into all the nitty-gritty of rocking our personal style, learning to accessorize, and what to do when nothing fits!

"But I don't have *time!*" you say.

I hear you, sister. My hope is that addressing the "why" of beauty in motherhood has motivated you to look at your day again, and see what you could re-prioritize so you can collect a few moments here and there to make progress on your journey. I know this takes discipline, and I'm preaching to the choir here… I just realized last week that if I check Facebook one less time each day, I have enough time to pluck my eyebrows each week!

What if I told you that making time for beauty only required five minutes here or there?

I have attempted to make this journey doable for you by placing "Mommy Makeover" moments in each chapter–action steps you can take in just five, ten, or twenty minutes that can help you embrace beauty in this season. The good news is, many of these things are one-time activities, like creating a style board, or choosing a personal color scheme, and they will equip you to make fast and fashionable decisions each time you get dressed!

I know time is a significant factor in whether we are practically able get ourselves together in the season of motherhood, but know that with small steps, and a commitment to *your* personal style (and not someone else's), you can embrace the beauty in every season of motherhood!

Seeing the Beauty in God's Design
{Loving Your Shape Today}

When God created Eve for Adam, the first words out of Adam's mouth were, "This at last is bone of my bones and flesh of my flesh;" (Genesis 2:23). My father-in-law, being a pastor, is familiar with the Hebrew in this verse and he tells me that our English does not do this passage justice. He says that when Adam saw the gift God had created for him, his response was one of such awe and excitement, a more literal translation might be "Shazam!" Adam was excited, and rightly so. God had done well—she was gorgeous and perfectly designed to complete mankind.

Yet we women pinch and pluck and criticize and critique and rarely give God glory for our beautiful design.

I sat across the table from three beautiful women at a dinner the other night. Each of them had given birth to a baby in the last 10 months. In fact, their beautiful bodies had together brought 11 children into the world! Each time I am with these women, I find myself appreciating their beauty—one has the darling-est nose and cutest grin, the other's hair is so full and becomingly cut, the third's coloring and eyes are truly stunning. Yet each of these women were bemoaning their weight, lack of style, and various other short-comings in the beauty department. I wanted to hold a magic mirror in front of them that would let them see what I saw when I looked at them. I wanted them to forget all the lies that the culture has fed them and see themselves as the exquisite creations that they are.

Who are we to declare that what He made isn't good? He designed our adolescent figures to grow in stature and our hips to widen in preparation for birthing children, our breasts to swell to provide them nourishment, and for our bodies to instinctively begin to pack on reserves when we become pregnant so that we will be nourished enough to bring that baby to a healthy birth weight, and then continue to grow it through nursing. This represents some fine planning and thoughtful design, but so often we resent our added weight and changing shape instead of praising Him for creating a plan that would so well provide for our children's growth!

Yes, many of us hang on to the baby weight longer than we wish—but I wonder if we're looking at this all wrong? Is the goal to slim down to our pre-pregnancy proportions between each pregnancy even healthy? If we are in the season of building babies with our bodies, maybe we should be more concerned about becoming too thin! I know that I was underweight before the birth of two of my children, and those pregnancies were very draining to my entire system. After my last pregnancy, I'm beginning to realize that it might actually be a good thing that I'm not back to my pre-baby weight—I won't start my next pregnancy as undernourished as my last ones. I wear the curves of motherhood, and isn't that something to take joy in, not resent? (Unless, of course, our tummy curve is related to diastasis recti which is a split in our abs that affects our entire health! This is treatable, my friend. Check out the information at the end of this chapter about fit2b.us!)

I mean, God could have designed us to pack weight on in

cubes or something—instead our weight simply enhances the curves He designed in a woman's body—the ones that cushion our laps for holding babies, and catch our husband's admiring eye. He designed our bodies to become downright voluptuous during our childbearing years. I think we need to start seeing the beauty in His design.

We need to learn to say with the Psalmist,

"I praise you because I am fearfully and wonderfully made; your works are wonderful, I know that full well."
Psalm 139:14 NIV

I've heard from so many moms that their biggest fashion challenge is that their waist is not the right size (yet) and they just can't be stylish until they've have lost some weight. And to you dear ones, may I whisper this:

You may not love your body, and maybe a certain amount of dislike for your figure is good motivation to make some healthy changes. But I will say (and, oops, what do you know, I've already lost the whisper), *one must accept one's figure in order to dress confidently.* I'm not trying to get you to be okay with being obese, because that's a health concern. But most of the mammas I know (including myself) worry about just a few inches here and there. I'm calling us to quit resenting what motherhood has done to our figures, and to realize that those extra pounds we blame on motherhood are actually part of God's beautiful design to nourish you and your baby well.

Fashion blogger, Christa Taylor[3] agrees:

"There is so much you can do now; putting off improvements 'until you lose 10 lbs' is not real life. Just own it, own your season of life and love the extra cush knowing it won't be forever and you're still a beautiful woman regardless of size or shape."

I have had my own struggles with body image. I am taller

than average, I have next-to-nothing cleavage, and despite being thirty, I'm bony and angular as a teenage boy in the throes of a growth spurt. I have such huge feet (size 12) that shoes are hard to find and I rarely have the luxury of purchasing anything beyond basic styles. These factors lead to as many wardrobe challenges as a short waist or 30 extra pounds or amazing hips. But these things are unchangeable about me, so I have to work with them.

I have learned to combat my angles with drapey styles and soft lines. I avoid certain styles because they don't work for my over-long legs, but I've also embraced the fun of using those cute little sundresses as tunics—it works on my long figure! (I have yet to figure out what to do with too-small boobs. Mine are nearly non-existent outside of lactation. In the words of my friend Rachel[4], "pregnancy was the best thing that ever happened to my boobs!").

One thing I won't tell you to do in this book is match your body type to a fruit, veggie, or shape. You know why? Because all that body shape advice stems from the belief that everyone is supposed to be an hour-glass figure. The "define your shape" approach spends most of the time teaching you how to get the illusion of an hourglass figure no matter what your God-given shape is, which I think is very demeaning. I reject this cookie-cutter approach to defining beauty, and instead I want to inspire you to embrace the shape you are and learn to style your body with a look you love. Defining a body shape doesn't really help in discerning what we love, it just dictates what we should wear if we want to look like something we're not.

I want you to wear something because you love it, not because a formula for your body shape tells you it will look good on you. The most flattering aspect of a woman's outfit is her confidence. When we accept our shape, and cue into that personal beauty detector that God wired deep down inside each of us—we can be the uniquely beautiful women we were created to be.

Another reason I'm not spending a lot of time on different body "types," is because as moms, our shape changes so regularly! Pre-baby I'm a banana. In pregnancy, I'm a watermelon. After pregnancy, I'm an apple (top heavy, if you know what I mean). The best technique for dressing your body shape is to love that body, whatever shape it is!

Maybe you're short. Maybe you're curvy. Maybe you're thicker—oops—than you meant to be. I'm not saying you should ditch the plan to cut out processed foods, but I do vote you accept what you have to work with in this season. Don't refuse to buy jeans until you've lost 3 sizes 'cause in the meantime you're gonna feel like a slob. Give yourself permission to focus on dressing well with the shape you are now.

How do you do this?

- Let your wardrobe inspiration come from images of models or friends with similar body styles. Don't fill your Pinterest board with photos of a gal who's half your height or weight— if that outfit works for her, it most likely won't work for you!

- Choose styles that leave room for growth or change. Are you trying to lose weight? After a few core pairs of pants, focus your energy and money on shirts and accessories that will still fit even after you drop the weight. Embrace styles like the tunic (See Chapter 9) which leave a lot of room for change.

- Make sure you're not equating personal style with personal worth. Despite how good clothes may make you feel, you are not what you wear. You are so much more.

Actually, clarifying my understanding of my identity in Christ has been one of the most important steps in my own fashion revolution. I was finally free to pursue my personal style when I quit seeing what I wore as a path toward acceptance and worth.

If you know who you are in Christ, you can wear anything (and any size!) and still feel secure and confident. And if you shop and dress for the size you *are* rather than the size you wish you could be, you can have style today, instead of only in your dreams.

Let's embrace today's beauty by clothing ourselves with the truth of His unconditional love for us. Accepting rather than resenting His design for your body during the season of motherhood will bless your husband, teach your kids the true definition of beauty, and be a testimony to all around you.

From that place of acceptance, we can move to clothing our mamma figures gracefully and with taste so that all will agree that God made something beautiful when He created a mother's body. That's what the rest of this book is about!

Tips for Stewarding Your Shape

One a side note, if it is time to lose some weight, I would love to point you to the resources that have helped me nourish and tone my mommy body so that it's in good shape for the season of motherhood that I'm in.

"Eat Fat Lose Fat" by Mary Enig

Crucial to maintaining a healthy weight is an understanding of which fats are essential to our body's nourishment, and getting enough of them in your diet. The fact is, if you are not giving your body the nourishment it needs, it will register that you are starving, and actually pack on whatever you do feed it as body fat as if in preparation for a famine. The ideas and recipes in this book can help you add good fats to your menu, allowing your body to be nourished and thus shed the reserves it no longer needs.

Real {Fast} Food

Whole foods and cooking from scratch are key ways to nourish our bodies well. If you're struggling to fit preparing healthy meals in with everything else you do as a mother, check out my cook book. It's full of time saving tips for the real food kitchen and includes all of my family's favorites from homemade yogurt to how to roast a whole chicken. Get your copy of Real {Fast} Food here (http://trinaholden.com/realfastfood).

Fit2B.us

Have you heard the news? Crunches, sit ups, and planks are the worst exercise for your mamma belly if your abdominal muscles are separated! You need to be doing tummy-safe exercises, which means diastasis-conscious and free of crunch-like motions and sit-ups! Bethany Learn, the founder of fit2b.us which streams TummySafe fitness routines to any internet ready device, is a certified personal fitness trainer with a bachelor's degree in exercise and sport science, and she's actually had kids and knows what exercises are good for your tummy and which ones aren't. She also knows how hard it can be to get to the gym as a mom, and how distasteful (and destructive!) many fitness videos are. Her online fitness studio at fit2b.us offers professional quality workout videos you and your whole family can benefit from in the comfort of your own home. I have been using her workouts for three months and have never felt better about my belly! You can use the code "FitwithTrina" and get $10 off your first three months!

Stand in front of the mirror and be honest with what you see. Despite the lumps, the thickness, the lack of resemblance to your teenage figure, you are a woman, and God made women beautiful. Before you turn away, smile and thank the Lord for the beauty in His design of your body. Next time you feel negative thoughts piling up about your appearance, turn the tide and focus on truth. You are beautiful right here, right now. You have a choice who you're going to believe for a definition of your worth as a mother—the culture or the God who created you.

Beauty in Balance
{Avoiding Extremes}

Before we dive into figuring out which hues and styles you were wired to love, I want to pause right here to make sure we keep this beauty quest in balance. Let's look at some extremes we can fall into in the area of external beauty…

Extreme #1

Some of my most informative years were spent in a Christian subculture that bound women to a standard of dress that was just plain ugly. I had these verses drilled into me:

> *"…women should adorn themselves in respectable apparel, with modesty and self-control, not with braided hair and gold or pearls or costly attire, but with what is proper for women who profess godliness—with good works."*
> *1 Timothy 2:9-10*

> *"Do not let your adorning be external—the braiding of hair and the putting on of gold jewelry, or the clothing you wear—but let your adorning be the hidden person of the heart with the imperishable beauty of a gentle and quiet spirit, which in God's sight is very precious."*
> *1 Peter 3:3-4*

These verses were used to support the message that adornment was sinful, and it was wrong to be unique, or in any other way attract attention with what you wore. The main idea was that our clothes were to be a barrier between us and the wandering eye of evil men. How tragic that something God created for joy was turned into a source of fear and anxiety!

I'm very grateful that the Lord has redeemed the area of fashion in my life from a burden that weighed me down with guilt and discouragement to a passion that fills me with joy and excitement. I've come to realize that what I wear is more than just a barrier between my body and the public, but can actually be a testimony to all I believe about beauty and its Creator.

I've learned that in order to get a balanced perspective on beauty, we need to look at everything God has said about getting dressed, and not just those two verses in the New Testament. As I delved into the scriptures in preparation for writing this book, I felt a building excitement as I began to see just how much God delights in beauty, and the role that outward adornment has played in His relationship with His people.

- The first clothes were made by God to provide for His children, Adam and Eve, after sin revealed their nakedness.

- The Psalmist uses clothes as a metaphor for how God covers our sins—"I will clothe her priests with salvation and her saints shall shout aloud for joy." Psalm 132:16

- Proverbs compares wisdom to necklaces and jewels—both are items of worth that set one apart from the crowd. (Prov. 3:15 and 8:11)

- Throughout the Old Testament, those who had been redeemed were repeatedly called to sing, dance, and adorn themselves as an outward expression of their deliverance. (Ezekiel 16: 13-14, Jeremiah 31:4)

- Multiple times in Revelation, God clothes those He has redeemed to show the world who belongs to Him. (3:5, 3:18, 4:4, 7:9, 19:8)

For those of us who have ever felt guilty focusing on our outward appearance, it's important that we see beauty was created by God and intended for our joy, and there's nothing inherently wrong with outward adornment. According to these scriptures, our appearance can actually function as part of our personal testimony. In fact, what we wear should be the outer-most layer of a soul clothed in salvation, beautiful because of redemption.

Extreme #2

The other imbalance many of us have struggled with is turning the quest for beauty into an idol. We put all kinds of effort into perfect hair, perfect nails, trendy styles, and expensive jewelry as our ticket to being accepted and feeling good about ourselves. I believe that this imbalance is what Peter and Paul were addressing in the above verses.

Not actually an order against braiding our hair, or wearing jewelry, as I had been taught, these verses are a warning against imbalance. They are a challenge to us women: "If you're gonna be known for your beauty, let it be more than skin deep." They warn us against putting all our efforts in the beauty department into our hair, skin, and accessories, and neglecting the inner woman—the heart—where true beauty flows from.

Is your beauty in balance? Is your outward adornment just one of several areas of your personhood in which you are seeking beauty, or is it the only one? Are you letting Him work in your heart, your attitude, your words, or are you using makeup and pretty clothes to cover up the fact that your insides are insecure and your spiritual life is being neglected?

Finding the Balance

Both extremes I've described grieve me. One denies God's passion for beauty and sees the celebration of His workmanship as a sin; the other turns the pursuit of beauty into an idol that will never satisfy.

I want to challenge you, sisters, to look at both ends of the spectrum and see where you may have leaned toward an imbalance. Look at the scriptures yourself to get a balanced view on the role beauty is to play in our lives. We need to remember that outward beauty is just one element of what makes us beautiful, and that our hearts need as regular attention as our eyebrows if we are to represent our Maker well.

What about Modesty?

I feel that modesty is cultural, situational, and a very personal topic. Your modesty standards are something you should decide between you, God, and probably your husband. I feel we should not be judging others on their level of modesty, nor letting others' opinions determine our standards. That being said, I'm gonna call you out and call you up:

If you have attempted to stand out by wearing a lower neckline, shorter skirt, or more revealing cut— Quit It. That's the cheap way to be noticed. I want to challenge you to dress for attention, not undress for attention. Be known for your class, not the amount of skin that you show.

And as to how much skin to show, I think we need to look at our bodies as a canvas with which to express the beauty God put inside each of us. A canvas without paint does not say much. So a body not properly clothed draws attention to the framework, instead of the outward layer God intended us to use to express ourselves and bring Him glory.

Don't believe the common myth that being modest means

being frumpy. Creative intentionality is all that is needed to bring today's trends up to the standard God has personally called you to.

Review again the verses in this chapter that address the act of getting dressed, or do your own word study with a concordance or your Bible app. Ask God to show you where your pursuit of physical beauty may be out of balance. Resolve that as you work to overhaul your wardrobe, you will not neglect the areas of your heart that may need a "makeover."

A Personal
Beauty Statement
{Finding Your Style}

We've agreed that God intended us to find joy in the beauty He created. But how do we celebrate our Creator with what we wear? By accepting what He has given us and learning to dress that body in a style that complements His unique design. Got big boobs? Don't be ashamed—He gave them to you. Long legs? This, too, is His workmanship. Short and small? Oh, sister! God has given us each something to celebrate and our bodies are yet another canvas on which to tell of His love for us. Wear your favorite color—every day if it makes you smile. God sure does. Glorify the norm and wear what you love even on weekdays.

So, what do we love? And how do we justify the time it can take us to discern our style? Doesn't that seem sort of selfish? Isn't our focus as mothers supposed to be about others? Yup. That's pretty much the definition of motherhood—serving others. But we serve better when we take care of our bodies. That's why we make time for good food, fitness, and sleep. But here I am asking you to add one more thing to that roster of what keeps mommy running like the Energizer bunny. Why? Because you can be doing all of the above but if you feel frumpy, your morale is going to be in the basement.

3 {Great} Reasons to
Define your Personal Style

1. Improves attitude! Wearing what you know you love gives your attitude, and thus your entire day, a boost. A woman who knows she's dressing herself well is confident and able to move beyond insecurities to focus on others.

2. Makes shopping faster! Knowing your style effectively narrows your options and keeps you focused in the store. For instance, I finally figured out I don't *do* yellow or green. Like, not really hardly ever at all. So that makes shopping faster because I can skip over anything in that category. At the thrift store, I take a big step past the yellows and dive into the pinks. And I completely ignore those green sweaters, even if the price is calling my name. I can canvas a store in half the time because I'm not looking at stuff I don't like anyway. You will actually free hours and hours of time in the future if you take the time to define your style now.

3. Makes dressing a joy! When you know what *you* love, and fill your closet with just those things, it makes the process of getting dressed a fun (and speedy) sport. Everything goes together with everything else because you've defined your personal style and you only buy items that fit in that category.

Sound too good to be true? Let me tell you, if someone had told me a year ago that shopping could actually be fast and fun, and that getting dressed could bring me joy every day, I'd have laughed in their face. "You don't understand," I'd have said, "I'm style-challenged. And I don't have time to figure this out. Some people have got it, some people haven't, and I'm one of the have-nots."

But then it happened for me. I experienced my own style revolution, despite my lack of faith. And now you can too. Here's four steps to take to get started on the journey:

1. Enlist Help

The first thing you have to do is realize that you are not an isolated island of fashion famine. Although the quest is for individual style, we need not be alone on the journey. Other moms are in the same boat, and being honest about where you're at, and where you need encouragement, can be the thing that leads you to your answers. Women are great brainstormers. Talking out your fashion questions and quandaries in community lets the power of a team enter the equation. One will recommend a book, another their favorite thrift store, a third might be wearing an outfit you adore, and can help you create the same look with something you already own.

I recommend shopping with your friends who have cute style. Having another's advice or perspective can be invaluable in helping us to figure out what works for us. My friends will pull out something I've over-looked and help me see its potential, or they can give me a thumbs down if I'm veering back toward my old habits of frump.

2. Become a Copycat

Next, we need to realize that it's okay to be a copycat. This one took me a while. I thought that because style was individual, it couldn't be based on someone else's style. Well, that's just not so. Actually, God designed us to be copycats in a way—He created us to be inspired and to want to reach for the beauty in His character and in His creation. Recreating beauty is a way we celebrate His creation and express the creative aspect of our own character. Seeing someone else's style that I love and patterning my outfits after her is actually a very efficient way to get the job done.

But we need to copy and be inspired by the right people. This was another place I floundered for a while. I have many friends and family members whom I consider stylish. But my efforts to let their outfits inspire my wardrobe always fell flat. We were different ages, different body types, or had different coloring. I was frustrated in my attempts to copy those around me because we were too unlike each other.

That's when I found Pinterest. In Hayley Morgan's wonderful book, "The No Brainer Wardrobe," she recommended creating a fashion pin board on Pinterest of outfits we love to create a guide for our wardrobe. As I built my pin board, I met the woman I was supposed to be getting inspiration from. She was the same height as me, same age, and had a similar build. And everything she wore also looked good on me. So I learned that if you're gonna copy, copy someone with the same build and age as yourself. If you're lacking a stylish twin sister, Pinterest makes a great stand-in.

3. Sort It All Out

After getting a visual on your personal style, you need to sort your closets mercilessly. I'm not saying you're gonna throw out the stuff that isn't you (if you're like me when I was at this stage, that would have left me with nearly nothing to wear!) but as an exercise, you need to show yourself what you love and what you hate in your wardrobe.

Forget how much you spent (or didn't spend), who gave it to you, or what occasion it really was perfect for, and let yourself sort your entire closet into two piles: Stuff I Love to Wear, and Stuff I Have to Wear Because I Have Nothing Better to Wear.

The first pile may be depressingly small, and the second discouragingly large, but this is a great first step. Because now you can look at the pile of stuff you love, and identify common themes of cut, color, and texture. This will guide you on future shopping trips. And you can look at the pile of stuff that makes you feel sick when you wear it, and tell yourself, sternly, you will never buy stuff in that category again (i.e., certain length skirts, that weight sweater, or that shade of pink).

If you're really serious about making a change, pack all the stuff you don't really like into a box. Put it in your closet. You don't have to get rid of it, in fact, you may need it tomorrow. But only let things that you love hang in your closet or lie in your drawers. That way, each time you look in your closet, you're reminded that you do have some sense of personal style, and those few items prove it.

Now, all that's left in your closet or drawers may be a few dressy pieces that are only fit to wear on a night out. What about everyday wear? Don't worry—I'm not telling you one must wear silk to clean toilets. You can use what you learn in this exercise to choose even casual clothes that still honor your personal style. Remember this is a process—don't let your malnourished wardrobe discourage you at this point.

4. Branch Out

Finally, it's time to try something new. The best place to do this is at the thrift store, or, better yet, a friend's closet. You want to be able to try out new colors, shapes, and fit without the burden of feeling like you have to love it because you spent that much on it.

It's called the $3 experiment. I did this the other day. I was shopping for cardigans. Preferably striped, because that was a recurring theme I was noticing in the outfits I was pinning on Pinterest. I saw an orange, striped cardigan for $3. I thought, "I don't wear orange. Or, at least, I don't think I do. I will be brave and buy an orange sweater and see if I *do* do orange." I mentally paired it with favorite stuff I had at home. Hmmm. It seemed to be fitting into my wardrobe okay. It was outside of my color comfort zone, but it wasn't in the don't-wear-this-ever-again spectrum, so I decided to give it a try.

Do you know by the time I got home I was in love? Absolutely smitten with an orange sweater. Who would have thought? You won't know unless you try. So borrow, beg, or buy cheaply, some items that are outside your comfort zone to help you discover what you love.

Now you have made the essential first steps in becoming one hot mamma. You have looked through Pinterest and your closet and seen some common themes emerging. Whether it was a suppressed love for western style, or a decided preference for punky details, those looks you *know* you love are your guideposts for the future. The amazing thing is, that even if you've ditched half your clothes in your sorting process, you may still have the makings for some great outfits with what you have, and only need to add a few accessories or core pieces to give the new you lots of options. That's what happened to me…

My Fashion Revolution

After building my first fashion pin board with styles I liked, I looked over it and realized some recurring themes.

- I saw immediately that I was very attracted to long skirts—despite being liberated from the frumpy ankle length styles I'd worn as a teen, I realized I still loved the long, willowy look of a tall woman in a full length skirt. There were many women out there wearing long, full skirts without being frumpy!

- I also noticed that I actually liked belts– especially thin ones, layered over cardigans or button-up shirts. My previous experience with belts had been completely utilitarian. Pinterest was showing me they were a great accessory and could add some sorely lacking definition to my current look.

- I kept being drawn to classic lines with modern punches of color and pattern. Stripes repeatedly caught my eye. So did feminine textures and artful layers.

My inner stylist was waking up, revealing she really did have opinions beyond basic neutrals! With a vision of the style of outfits I wanted to create fresh in my mind, I ran upstairs to sort through my closet. After a survey I came up with a surprisingly short list of items I needed to complete my new look:

1. A skinny belt

2. A long skirt

3. A pair of riding boots

I picked up a belt for a quarter at the thrift store the next week. Then I found a ginormous dress that I chopped and fitted into a flared, floor-length maxi skirt. The boots were the biggest challenge because of the size of my feet, but my husband helped me unearth a brand with a size I fit and a style I loved, and gave them to me for Christmas.

Just these few items revamped my entire wardrobe! I found the shorter skirts I already owned looked fresh and trendy when paired with the boots. The new belt added definition to outfits that had previously been too loose and frumpy, and when I wore my floor-length brown skirt I felt like I was finally being true to my personal style.

Your Turn

I believe that you are not that far from your own fashion revolution if you will take the time to catch a vision for what you love, and let that picture guide you in your future choices.

In the next chapter we're going to dig even deeper into your inner fashionista and create a personal color scheme to further guide you toward defining your style.

Mommy Makeover

Here's your homework. These are the longest "Mommy Makeovers" in the book because they're foundational, and you'll really only have to get this deep and dirty once. After this, you'll *know* what you love and deep closet sortings will be a thing of the past.

Take 20 minutes to call a girlfriend whose fashion sense you admire. Share with her that you're trying to grow in this area. Tell her what you love about her style, and ask her if she'll be your cheerleader. You can even—gasp—ask her if she'll pray with you about this. If she thinks you're crazy for praying about fashion, share with her how important you've come to believe beauty is for moms (review Chapter 1!).

Spend 20 minutes this week building a style wardrobe on Pinterest, or, if you already have one, 10 minutes analyzing it, pruning, and identifying some common elements. For more help with this step in defining your style, check out Hayley's book, "The No Brainer Wardrobe."

Spend 20 minutes throwing all your clothes into two piles— "love it!" and "not so much." Hang the results of this sorting session on opposite sides of the closet so you have a clear visual on what you're shooting for.

Instagram a photo of your cleansed closet with the hashtag #MomsEmbracingBeauty to celebrate!

Extra credit: Next time you're shopping, spend less than $10 on an item that is a little outside your comfort zone so you can figure out if it's actually something you love.

Find links, resources, videos and more at
http://trinaholden.com/embracing-beauty/extras/

What's Your Favorite Color?
{How to Choose a Personal Color Scheme}

What's your favorite color? Caution: This is a trick question. At least, it was for me!

Color is yet another area that God intended to give us joy, but too often we let others' rules and guidelines dictate what we wear, rather than simply choosing the colors we love best.

- We listen to the science of skin tone and hair color and so we never let redheads wear pink.

- We listen to the style forecast and don mint green and grape even though these colors (and their corresponding flavors) make us gag.

- And we sometimes make the mistake of thinking that the colors we chose for our living room décor must also be the pallet we base our wardrobe on.

We get stuck in defining our personal style when we adopt others' rules about what colors we should or should not wear, and forget that color is a very personal subject.

In my first home, I dressed the couch in green and blue, the bed in green and blue, the walls, curtains, dishes, and shelves all with green and blue. Because green and blue, I knew, made me feel peaceful and at rest.

When I went clothes shopping, I tended toward the same color scheme, because I thought that's what I loved. My wardrobe matched my house: blues, greens and neutrals. It was all rather blah. In fact, some days if I wore the right outfit, I blended into the couch and became completely camouflaged!

I thought I was wearing the right colors, but my wardrobe often made me feel green about the gills. I never seemed to be able to create an outfit with any pizzazz…probably because everything in my closet had about as much personality as a clump of moss.

Gradually I realized this was because I had made the mistaken assumption that the same colors I loved for décor should be the colors I wore.

Silly me.

It was my thrift shopping addiction that led me to realize what was missing in my wardrobe. I had this bad habit of buying something just because it was cheap, even if it wasn't what I thought was my favorite color.

One day this poor habit led me to buy a silky, shimmery blouse that had splashes of red and dark pink. I said it was totally *not* me, but I was desperate for a fancy blouse to wear to some occasion and it fit and was cheap, so I bought it.

Then the weirdest thing happened. I wore the blouse and felt wonderful. I wore it again and received several compliments. In fact, each time I wore that loud, fun blouse, I felt a little bit more right about it.

Then I found a red shirt on sale. I *never* wear red. But it was *really* on sale.

I caved.

And it, too, became a favorite.

Finally I noticed I actually felt better and more confident in warmer tones, and that one of the secrets to feeling good in my clothes was as simple as admitting that my favorite paint color was different than my favorite shirt color.

So, I ask you again, what is your favorite color? Have you been wearing your favorite color, or have you been wearing your couch cover?

How do certain colors make you feel? Red is often associated with excitement, blue with peace. Green is a restful color, orange is celebratory. Do you love to be surrounded by exciting colors or peaceful colors?

We enjoy different colors in different settings and uses. The color you would paint a wall, may not be the color you would wear to feel confident, and your favorite color for couch cushions may be on the other side of the spectrum from the color you'd choose to wear on vacation.

I've spoken with several of my friends on this subject and we have all been surprised to realize that the colors we like most to be surrounded with (i.e., wall paint, furniture, or the colors we use in our blog design) are usually on the opposite side of the color wheel from the colors we enjoy wearing.

Try this: Stand in front of your closet and imagine it's your birthday and you're going out. Which outfit are you drawn to that matches your mood? That's the color you should focus on, more often than not, when you're shopping and creating outfits.

Recognizing the colors you love to wear is the first step in creating a personal color scheme. My friend, Rachel, is going to talk us through the next steps, because she was the one who first introduced me to the concept of a personal neutral.

Finding Your Personal Neutral
{by Rachel Hurd[5]}

"Personal neutral" means a color, or colors, that work with nearly every item in your wardrobe, complementing them and adding that finishing touch to your outfits. Your personal neutral can (and probably will) change with the seasons, years, and styles, yet identifying your current personal neutral will help to streamline your shopping process immensely.

Now, "neutral" can be a bit of a misleading term; in this particular case, it doesn't necessarily mean black, white, grey, cream, brown or navy. It can mean those colors, and also green, purple, citron, tomato, burgundy, mint, coral, etc., etc! Whatever color(s) go with nearly every item of clothing in your wardrobe will be your personal neutrals. For some folks, it's one of the traditional standards (black or brown) plus a fun color that draws their eye every time they're shopping. For other folks (like me), it's bright/trendy colors that carry over the seasons and lend a little excitement to wardrobe staples. Generally you will have two personal neutrals, but that's not a hard-and-fast rule. Follow your eye and have a blast!

How to Choose Your Personal Neutral

Your personal neutral is probably already hanging around your house somewhere, just waiting to be discovered. I generally send people to their jewelry/accessories drawer first, since that is the place that most folks feel as though they have some expression of their personal tastes. What color(s) do you see in predominance there—red, purple, orange, turquoise? If that color still makes you smile when you see it, you've already found one of your personal neutrals!

If all that you see in your jewelry box is silver or gold, though, you have the fun task of choosing a personal neutral! First, identify your chosen metal. If you're a silver person, you probably wear more black/white combinations (this is just a guess—I know that there will be that one person out there who totally throws off the curve!); if you're a gold person, warmer tones most likely dominate your closet.

If you like (and wear) silver jewelry, consider these colors:

- Red (burgundy, tomato, coral, maroon, etc.)
- Purple (lavender, eggplant, plum, violet, etc.)
- Blue (ink, cobalt, sky, turquoise, royal, baby, etc.)
- Green (seafoam, mint, olive, forest, kelly, lime, etc.)
- Pink (neon, rose, salmon, fuchsia, etc.)

These all go well with black, cream, grey and white, so you can choose one of these as your basic personal neutral if you don't want to go too crazy.

If your jewelry box is primarily filled with gold, you can choose any of the colors above, along with:

- Orange (tangerine, vermillion, pumpkin, amber, etc.)
- Yellow (citrine, saffron, goldenrod, pale, etc.)

After you've had a glance through your jewelry box, take a look through your closet. Do you see mostly denim, black, and white? Those are great building blocks to a versatile wardrobe, but they're crying out for some personalization! Take a look around your house. Is there a particular color that you use often and find your eye drawn to? Chances are, that's a variation of your personal neutral. It's a shade that makes you smile and makes you happy to be alive. Shouldn't you wear that color at least several times a week?

Once you have chosen your person neutral (or two— I like to have two completely different shades to add depth and interest to my wardrobe), head over to your nearest Target/Walmart/superstore that sells clothes and pick up a couple of camisoles or tanks in those colors. (Tanks and camis are some of the hardest items to thrift for, since they are such workhorses in most ladies' wardrobes, so I usually suggest that you spring for new ones. However, they are generally quite inexpensive and will last you years if you launder them well.) If you just chose one personal neutral in addition to a true neutral, try to find two different shades to play around with—variety is the spice of life! Experiment with saturation and shade... if blue is your neutral, try turquoise with your browns and royal with your blacks. Or reverse them! The main thing is, have fun with your neutrals.

The next step is to use them! When you pull out your denim skirt and black sweater, toss on the turquoise tank instead of your usual white shirt. Layer your new tanks and camis under, over, and around your basics and get used to the way your new personal neutral looks on you. Don't like the shade? Try another! It takes a little while (especially if you're starting from scratch) but it's worthwhile. And you'll feel fabulous while you play around with color!

What's the benefit of having a personal neutral? It eliminates the guess work while thrifting! If you already know that nearly every item in your wardrobe goes with green, you like green, your jewelry coordinates with green, etc., you can pass right on by the yellows, pinks and purples, thereby streamlining the process. Of course, I try not to close myself off to the possibility of a changing neutral, but a quick thrift-store run for new accessories isn't necessarily the time to experiment. When you want a sure-fire choice to add interest to your wardrobe, go with your personal neutral! It will make everything easier.

Once you've chosen your shade (and remember, it can be your neutral for summer only, if you like more variety), keep a lookout for accessories, shirts, bottoms, jewelry, etc., in that color. Your whole wardrobe will start to come together and it will be effortless for you to throw on a fabulous scarf and feel completely put together.

So, let's review the reasons to identify your personal neutral and craft a personal color scheme:

- Your clothes always coordinate
- You can shop twice as fast
- Your clothes will make you feel happy
- It makes it easier for your friends to buy you presents

Are you convinced? Okay, let's do this thing!

Using Rachel's tips, look in your closet, drawers, and jewelry box to identify a color you obviously love. Look deeper to identify the outfits you create that generally revolve around that color. Now imagine if you had another shirt, tank, scarf, pair of pants, or belt in said color, and how many *new* outfits you could create with your current clothes if you bought items that went with your color scheme.

There's a saying "if the shoe fits, buy it in every color." I have a new fashion phrase for you: If the color fits, buy it in every shoe—or, in every accessory. You should own belts, scarves, tanks, necklaces, etc., in your favorite shades, allowing you to complete any ensemble with colors you love. Learn to shop within your personal color scheme to create endless outfit combinations that never clash.

Share a picture of you rocking your personal neutral with the hashtag #MomsEmbracingBeauty.

A Firm Foundation
{In Which We Mention Unmentionables}

Perhaps the most neglected part of a mommy's wardrobe is her bras. Once we enter motherhood what was once ornamental and pretty low-maintenance becomes utilitarian and a daily challenge to keep under control. They swell, bulge, and grow out of anything they fit, all while gaining a nasty attitude and extreme sensitivity. Oh, and they leak. What's up with that?! Suddenly, instead of an asset, we have a liability hanging off our chest, waiting for the next chance to embarrass us. Sisters, this ought not so to be.

You are beautiful, and your breasts, full or floppy, are one of the details God added to give you curves and appeal. Let's get those gals back in line so we can enjoy them, shall we? This is gonna take a little effort and investment, but the results will be amazing.

Seeing as most of my bras have come from clawing through nasty girdles and vintage brassieres at the thrift store, I was fairly certain this was an area of my wardrobe I'd been neglecting, so, in the name of book research, I bravely went and got a fitting.

This was one of the most amazing experiences of my life. Not just because this conservatively-raised girl was overwhelmed walking into a store full of nearly-nude models and lots and lots of undies, but because of what happened in the dressing room. After an awkward fitting with the sales lady (mostly awkward because she was willing to measure me over my clothes right in the middle of the store with mall-goers walking by the floor-to-ceiling windows—I asked her if we could go to the back), I slipped into the dressing room with two little tangles of elastic and foam padding (remember how small I told you I am?). I self-consciously slipped one of them on, and suddenly I knew why people spend $70 on a bra. There, strapped around my chest was the most comfortable bra I'd ever worn, and best of all, it made me look amazing. Little old me! Now, I promise I didn't choose the Bonus Push-Up Bombshell style. It's just that this bra, perfectly fitted to me and high quality, did what a bra is supposed to do—lift and support. Oh, my. I was smitten. With myself. Which was another rather awkward moment, but all for a good cause. I came out of the dressing room armed with the experience needed to convince my readers to invest in this area of their wardrobe.

A good bra can remind you that God did, indeed, make you beautiful. Not that you're not beautiful without one, but our culture likes well-rounded, supported boobs, so getting a bra that makes you feel comfortable and culturally acceptable is a great way to start your day and your mommy makeover.

But what if you can't get away or out of the house for such frivolous things as measuring your boobs? Or what if the average boutique doesn't carry your size? Well, I have good news. I'm not gonna be the one to educate you. Nope, I'm gonna let an expert handle this topic. This is where I hand the mic over to my friend, DeeDee, who was trained to measure and fit bras during the time she worked at a large department store. She kindly shares all the inside secrets to a getting a flattering fit in the convenience of your own home.

How to Choose the Right Bra
{by DeeDee Justice}

Boobs, nipple, breast… I just kind of wanted to get those words out there before I continued so the giggles are over with now. It's just a part of the body, so chill.

I really do not know many women who like to shop for bras. They love to shop for dresses or jewelry or shoes, but never bras. That's typically because there are a million styles or you don't know what size to look for and it's sometimes embarrassing to ask for help in that area. Please don't be embarrassed! They are just boobs and every woman has them. Plus, if you fit them properly, your outfit that you put over them will look even more amazing!

Why They Are Necessary...

Just for your information, if you wear a size double d, the combined weight of your breasts can be 25 pounds. Seriously! 25 pounds! Crazy, right? If that is not properly supported it can do serious damage to your back. Even if your cup size is not that big (even an A cup,) you need to have plenty of support. If you have ever felt little twinges of pain in the very top portion near where they connect to your chest, that is breast tissue ripping, and the only way to fix that is through surgery. This is especially something to think about if you are exercising. If you are trying to purchase a sports bra, jump around. If they are bouncing, you either need a smaller size or need to wear two at once.

How They Should Fit...

This is the part that everyone wants to know about. What size am I??? You will need a partner and a flexible measuring tape for this. First, you measure just above any part of the bust, around your body, and to take the measurement you need to drop your arms to your side, so that the tape rests near your underarms. (This is why you need a partner because it is impossible to take the measurement yourself with your arms down.) The first measurement should be taken with the tape snug. Not so tight that you have skin rolling over it, but pretty fitted. The reason you measure above the bust instead of right below is that your ribs can protrude slightly, causing the measurement to be off.

The second measurement is going to go over the largest part of your chest, which is typically at the nipple line. This is going to be a little bit looser measurement. It will still be touching the skin all the way around, just not as snugly. Make sure to drop your arms to your sides on the second measurement as well.

Measurement one is your band size. Band sizes only come in even numbers so if you got 35.5 round up to 36 and if you got 34.5 round down to 34. If you are right in the middle at 35" (or 33" or 37", etc.), I would suggest that you try on both sizes. It will depend on the style which size will work better for you. To find the cup size you simply subtract the first measurement from the second measurement. The number of inches will determine the cup size, i.e., 1"=A, 2"=B, 3"=C, 4"=D, 5"=DD/E and etc. (By the way, DD and E are the same, DDD and F are the same, and DDDD and G are the same. It will depend on the brand which they prefer to put on the tag.) So if your measurements are 32" and 36", you would be a 32D. Sounds simple enough right? It generally is with the exception that all styles are not created equal. This is why you *must* try them on in the store and make sure it is fitting properly.

When you are trying on a bra, it is recommended that you hook the bra on the center hook unless it is that one week per month you are retaining water weight. This will allow you to be able to loosen the band on that week and allow it to be tightened once it inevitably stretches out a bit. Another option is to try it on the loosest hook so you will have even farther to take it in when it stretches out. After you have it on, you want to make sure the straps are tightened just enough where you can still fit two fingers underneath it. For the cups, you need to reach all the way in and lift your entire breast up and into the center to make sure the underwire is not on any breast tissue. Make sure you are standing straight up, not sitting or leaning over when you are adjusting the cups.

The first part of checking if it is fitting correctly is checking the band. Eighty percent of your support is going to come from the band, not the straps, so if it is wrong, it's a big problem. When looking at the front, the center part between your cups should be laying flat against the body. If it is poking out, there is a good chance the cups are too small or the band is too big. The underwire should also be flat against the body and not laying on any breast tissue. This is especially true on the sides of the cups. The underwire should be behind all of the breast tissue or there is a good chance you are bruising yourself on a daily basis.

If you have what looks like back fat hanging over the back of the band, there's a good chance the band is just too tight. If that's the case, it doesn't matter if you are a size 2 or 22, it will not look attractive. On the other hand, if the band is riding up in back, the band is typically too loose.

Onto the cups… it should be one seamless line from the bottom of the underwire to your neck. If there is a gap between your breast and the cup, the cup is too big. If you have spillage, which is where the breast tissue is bulging over the top of the cup, the cup is too small.

Not All Boobs Are Equal...

One thing that most people don't talk about is that, unless you have had surgery to make them that way, your boobs will not be even. Some people are lucky enough to have them be close enough that you cannot tell while others can be several cup sizes different. Typically it is just one cup size or less and there are some really quick and easy ways to fix this.

First, take measurements just on the larger breast side from your sternum to your backbone. You always want to fit the larger side because you need to have as much support as possible.

Next, start with a molded cup bra. This is just one that has a form already. Some full busted women are concerned this is going to add more to them, but that is not the case. It is just creating a nice form and also preventing everyone in the room from knowing you are cold. Some molded-cup bras come with a little pocket and inserts which make the next steps much easier.

You also want to get familiar with inserts. They can be filled with air, water, gel, or just foam. As far as which you use, it's simply personal preference. If there is a large difference between the two breasts you might consider the gel or water, just to give you the weight to match the other side.

To make the breasts look even pull out the insert on the larger side and make sure that side fits well. On the smaller side keep the insert in the pocket provided. If you are purchasing one without the pocket, just put the insert in the bottom of the cup along the underwire in the deepest part of the cup. You then want to reach in and pull the entire breast up and in like you normally would. If there is still a gap in the cup, add a second insert just on top and above the first one. To hold it in, consider purchasing dress tape which can be attached to the insert and the bra.

Proper Care...

Bras should not be worn more than one day in a row. It takes a minimum of 24 hours for the elastic to go back to its original form. If you do choose to wear it more than one day at a time, just know that it is going to die faster. Because of this, you should have a minimum of 3 good bras at any given time. If you only have 3 though, they will typically only last about 6 to 8 months on average. A really good brand might last a year, if you are lucky.

When you wash them, they should always be either hand washed or they can go in the washing machine on a gentle cycle, preferable in a lingerie bag. Make sure all hooks are hooked if they are going in the washing machine. To dry, they should be laid flat. Never invert the cups or you will get creases that are nearly impossible to get out.

Where To Go...

If you are not confident enough to fit yourself, that is perfectly all right. There are many places where trained professionals in this type of thing are waiting to help you. One I know that will measure and fit you correctly is Dillard's, because that's where I used to work. The Certified Lingerie Fitters there actually have to take a course, fit a certain number of people and then take a test to be certified, so you know they know what they are doing. Some others that I have heard can measure you are Frederick's, J.C. Penney's, and Victoria's Secret. I would be cautious about the last one though, because when I went in, they measured me incorrectly.

In our quest for a well-fitting bra, it's important to remember (not resent) that God made us each unique. Your journey will be different than mine because our boobs are different! (duh!) Here's a handful of experiences that my friends shared with me that showed me just how many ways you can take to finding the proper foundation for your wardrobe.

"So, a few months ago a friend told me I should go get a fitting, and I finally bit the bullet and did it. Thankfully I roped a good friend into coming along for moral support. And now... while I had been actually wearing the right size, I feel like a NEW WOMAN! A high quality bra is amazing and even some of my shoulder/neck pain is less! My husband loves the results so much I think he'd be willing to work an extra job just to buy a few more! In fact, when I came home with 2 tan ones - being sensible and making my money work practically - he was disappointed that I hadn't spent the extra $17 on the frilly ones!"
—Confidently Carrying

"Oh my goodness! I was just fitted for the first time two weeks ago. I went to [a store with] professional fitters. One of them spent two hours with me (no charge) and I was amazed at what I learned after spending the last 30+ years wearing a bra! My size is not what I thought, and I am SO much more comfortable and happy with my appearance now! ...My fitting experience wasn't invasive at all. I always hesitated because I wasn't sure if I'd have to bare myself. But they measured me in my clothes, and only saw me in the bras if I asked them to come in. It took so long because I was convinced I could not be the size they measured. When I finally decided to give it a try, it was a perfect fit!"
—Double D Diva

"I actually just bought new bras recently and for the first time in years went with underwires. HUGE difference. Since my bust is so... ample I was afraid they'd be just too, too much, but the opposite is true. I actually go down a dress size with these bras... mainly because the support is there."
—Blessed Beyond a B

"I'm with the bustier bunch on this one. Stores never carry my size. Online shopping is a life saver. I just buy a bunch in what sizes I think I am (based off of measurements) and try them all on."

–Becky Bosom

Boobs at Work
{How to Not Cry Over Spilled Milk}

Why are we talking about lactation in a book about fashion? Because I'm committed to leaving no stone unturned to make sure you feel glamorous as a mom.

Boobs are the most challenging to clothe in the season of nourishing wee ones. Again, this is an area you may need to spend more money than you are used to spending on yourself, but I say again, it's worth it. Think how heavy your breasts are and how often you snap and unsnap a nursing bra on a newborn's feeding schedule. Equipment that works that hard deserves more of an investment!

Layered Protection

There are three layers of protection I recommend putting between you and the embarrassment of leaking.

Layer One: A Good Nursing Bra

Now, although the idea of getting underwear at the thrift store may wig you out, I will say that I have found some beautiful, brand new, high quality nursing bras second hand. My theory as to why I've had such good luck in the second-hand market with nursing bras is that many woman will invest in a good bra, but only end up nursing for a few weeks. So, that's one place to look. But, if you're picky about what color, what style, and what snap features you like, you're gonna have to broaden your search.

My readers and friends have recommended Cake Lingerie, Belle Materna, and Bravado Designs.

Layer Two: Great Nursing Pads

Although many of us resort to stuffing our shirts with burp rags, one shouldn't leave home without a handful of good nursing pads. Washable are preferable to most because they're environmentally friendly and are less likely to incur breast infections than their disposable, plastic lined counterparts.

Friend and blogger, Beth[6], recommends Bamboobies[7].

"I'm a MAJOR leaker for the first 6+ months. I've tried a ton of various cloth ones, but the ONLY ones that work for me are Bamboobies. They are fantastic. Bamboo absorbs way more than cotton. I throw a cotton pad in and my shirt will be soaked down one side in just one nursing session, but the Bamboobies? They do the job. Plus they're thin, and shaped like a heart which makes them shaped to the roundness of your breast, and they don't show under clothes. I love them."

Layer Three: Layering Accessories

Scarves cover a multitude of boob-related issues. Drape a leak, fill in a neckline that's gaping with cleavage, and double as a nursing cover. I love keeping a scarf handy to draw attention away from the girls if they're not behaving!

Most women swear by nursing tanks. I usually get by with at least one tank, nursing style or otherwise, layered under whatever else I'm wearing. I like them long, so when I lift up in the front, I'm not exposing my backside to the world or a chilly breeze. When my friend, Rebekah[8], reviewed Bravado Design's "Essential Nursing Tank"[9] on her blog, she said she loved their tank because it has "a full bra built into the tank top. Bravado doesn't size their tanks by small, medium, or large. They use actual bra measurements so you are sure to get a perfect fit!"

If you're not used to layering your outfits, now's the time to embrace this as the fun and practical art form that it is. We'll talk more on this subject in Chapter 8: "The Art of Layering."

Bonus Tip: When I was three weeks into nursing my first-born and dealing with the sopping mess of learning to nurse, a woman I didn't even know came up to me at a conference and thoughtfully shared this tip: since the heaviest leakage occurs during let-down, you can greatly reduce the amount of "spilled milk" by applying pressure to the nipple that's not in use during the first few minutes of nursing. This effectively slows the flow of breastmilk and keeps you from soaking through every pad you've got at every nursing. This pressure can be applied discreetly with the inside of the arm that is probably already in the general vicinity as you assist your baby in latching on or stroke his/her baby cheek. This works even in public—no one need know that your arm is doing double duty. *wink* If you experience a let-down outside of nursing (which happens more often in the first few weeks of nursing–sometimes all it takes is hearing your baby cry!), you can simply cross your arms casually across your chest, and keep smiling. Everything is under control!

Even with the best nursing bras, though, we can get tired of all the necessary hardware. Take my friend Claire's[10] advice:

"When my husband and I go out on our date night, or when I have a chance to go out by myself for a few hours, I try to make a point of wearing a non-nursing bra. It may sound ridiculous, but it gives me a little time to feel like I am not just a mom and a milk machine."

Finally, don't neglect frilly, fun pieces in your lingerie drawer during this season! The bedroom is the perfect place to make the most of those engorged beauties! I love stores like Rue 21 where I can spend $6 on something colorful and festive in whatever size I am at the time.

Ladies, it's time to start loving your boobs again. Take care of them and they can start being an asset instead of a liability!

Find a friend, daughter, or even your husband (although I suggest him as a last resort because men find this kind of task distracting *wink*) and take your measurements according to DeeDee's instructions. Next, get online and do a little window shopping. If you find a brand, style, and price that fits your budget, make a good bra your next fashion purchase.

Expect Great Things
{A Rebellion Against Frump in Pregnancy}

Pregnancy is the one season of our life in which everyone—God, your husband, the culture, and your mom—agree that you should gain weight. Now that, girlfriend, is a reason to celebrate! But even with the lowering of expectations about your waistline, pregnancy presents its own challenges.

- You are gaining weight every month, but it goes in fits and starts, while never resembling the pattern of your past pregnancies. (Just 'cause you've done this before doesn't mean you have an advantage.)

- You have less energy for shopping trips or marathon try-everything-on-in-the-closet sessions. If you get really sick during your pregnancy, nothing but P.J.'s makes any practical sense.

- Comfort becomes more important than ever, as previously low maintenance areas of your body become tender and touchy.

Yet it remains important that we embrace beauty in this season, too. If we resent how we look when pregnant, that attitude can grow into resenting pregnancy in general. It can be hard to see our children the way God does (as a blessing) when we resent what their advent did to our bodies and sense of style!

I have struggled in this area during past pregnancies, feeling very strong aversion to memories and photos of my pregnant self. Looking back, I know it had more to do with the fact that I was struggling to dress that belly, than with the weight gain itself. Since then I have vowed that in future pregnancies I would use what I have learned about my personal style to reject the frump and dress that belly well.

In pregnancy, I truly feel that comfort should be the first priority. But that doesn't have to mean stretch pants and your husband's sweatshirts the whole time—not if you know your favorite colors and are willing to learn to accessorize. Here are my favorite pieces for pregnancy:

- **Scarves**. It's a principle of design that a person's eyes will rest on whatever is in the foreground, or closest to the eyes. If you're feeling less than at ease with the way your belly or boobs are sticking out there, put something else up front, like a bright or textured scarf. This simple length of fabric can transform a simple jeans and shirt combo into a put-together ensemble.

- **Tunic-style tops**. I hate it when things don't meet in the middle—especially if we're talking pants and tops. Avoid this problem entirely by choosing tops that drape well beyond your waist. If you feel like you look like a bloomin' tent, then add my next favorite maternity accessory—

- **Belts**. You do have a waist, girlfriend! It's just moved North. Define the narrowest part of your torso with a belt. Sequins or leather, thick or thin, belts are a great way to bring balance and finish off an outfit.

- **Layering tanks**. These are an essential layer for many outfits, but are also a way to add variety to your wardrobe. Find a brand you love, then go ahead and get yourself as many colors as you can afford. I'm serious.

This is a Splurge Zone, ladies, and you won't regret it. A sturdy, long tank top is going to be your best friend well beyond your pregnancy. I don't go for the ones with a shelf bra simply because those preggo boobs can drag a neckline too low for comfort. Instead, I find a brand that focuses on giving me the length to cover my belly, and let my bra do the work of supporting the girls.

Tips for Hopeful and First Time Moms...

Don't buy maternity clothes until you actually start to gain weight. Every woman's body carries their baby weight differently. It's no good buying those maternity jeans until you find which band actually feels comfortable on your 6-month bulge. Also, you may be surprised just how big your breasts will grow, requiring totally new sizes up top, as well! Wait to go shopping until you actually begin to grow out of your normal size.

Maternity clothes are sized more generally than regular clothes. Most brands simply define things relatively as small, medium, large, and extra large. The size you are in normal clothes will not be any help here. You must be prepared to try on pants and dresses outside of your normal comfort zone, and expect it to change. A lot. As I go through my pregnancies I find I wear a different size for each trimester. I usually start in what is a medium in most brands, grow into a large, and eventually hit the extra large sizing. Do not panic about those labels—this is all very natural!

Be aware that you will probably gain several bra cup sizes even before baby gets here and you start producing milk. Don't try to stuff yourself into your old bras—this will be painful and may damage milk ducts. Spend the time and money you have to get at least two comfy bras that support you well through this season (see Chapter 6 for fitting tips and favorite nursing bra brands).

Tips for Returning Champions...

My personal policy for maternity fashion is "In whatsoever state I am...buy maternity clothes."

In the past I have put cute maternity outfits I liked back on the rack 'cause I was nowhere near a need for elastic waist bands that month, and didn't even want to think about wearing maternity clothes. But now, having endured three pregnancies in frumpiness, wearing colors I hated and pants that were too short, I never pass on an opportunity to add a good piece to my maternity wardrobe.

Now, of course, I shop almost exclusively at thrift stores, and I'm not anywhere near average, meaning it's only a few times a year that I actually find something that's long enough for my legs and fits my criteria. So I don't have a huge closet full of cute maternity clothes. No, but I do have a nice bin of choice maternity pieces stored away thanks to local thrift stores and my Company Policy.

You mammas who have "been there" can shop in advance like this because you have some idea of what your size range is when you are pregnant. You also know what type of waist line you like in your jeans and what length skirts on your dresses.

The Core Outfit Strategy

Every pregnancy will be different, with your body a different size in a different season of the year. The pieces you loved from your last pregnancy may not work at all for this one. I recommend choosing a foundational look for a month at a time, and get a few core pieces you can mix and match.

For example, say you're in your first trimester and it's summer. A look you may like is shorts and a flowy baby doll blouse or tunic. You'll want to get two or three pairs of shorts that fit you now but with a bit of room to grow, and a few tops. To create a variety of looks from these core pieces, accessorize and mix it up with necklaces, different colored tank tops, and a few pairs of cute sandals. Beware of the tendency to wear something that's too big now, just because you'll grow into it. Set your larger blouses aside and dress the size you are this month.

Or, let's say it's winter and you're in your eighth month. Your best fashion friend is a pair of jeans that will comfortably stay up on your hips. Beg, buy, or borrow at least 2 pairs of comfy jeans and then look for the largest, drapiest, comfiest, stretchiest shirts in your favorite colors. Add variety to this shirt and jeans combo with cardigans (maternity or otherwise) belted above your belly, scarves around your neck, and structured jackets that offset your new proportions. These are casual looks that will get you through a day of errands, chores, and setting up the nursery.

When you need to dress up, trade the jeans for dress slacks, or, better yet, get yourself a maxi dress in a neutral color. You can wear one of these great inventions through your entire pregnancy and change the look each time you wear it by adding different accessories. If you have a special occasion to attend, like a wedding, wait until right up close to the date of the occasion to do your shopping so you'll be sure to fit your investment on the special day.

Dressing your pregnant body can be a challenge, but also a source of real joy and fulfillment as you embrace the gift of a child and the beauty of God's design that will bring that baby into the world. Don't let this season defeat your style. Don't compromise just because you have nothing else to wear. Make the effort to find those core pieces and accessories that will love you and your belly. You can be one hot mamma if you make a plan and stick with what you know you love.

Solutions for the Season of Nursing

I love breastfeeding. But. Dressing my body when I'm in

milking mode can be more challenging than pregnancy! Why? Well, for one thing, lactation lasts longer than pregnancy for me, so I get plumb weary of it. Not many stylish dresses include easy nursing access, so for months on end I can only glance wistfully at my favorite dresses in my closet while I search yet again for a skirt and top combo that match and will provide nursing access. There is never the simplicity of just pulling on a dress, it's always tops and bottoms, tops and bottoms. Add to that, my body is still a different shape every month, and... I leak. Yeah, clothing oneself while lactating is indeed a challenge.

I think our best strategy in this season is to continue to define our style and our personal color scheme so that when we put together an outfit we can focus solely on fit. If we know what we love then we can simply concentrate on building layers with what works that month.

As I suggested for pregnancy, decide on a core look that works for you right now, and work to create variety and lots of choices within that style. Skirts work better than dresses right now, so figure out what length you love (I like either full length, or right above the knee—nothing in between looks right on these long legs!) and what style top balances that out. (The fuller the skirt, the more fitted your top should be). If you have three skirts and three tops that all coordinate, that's a total of nine different looks that you can switch up even more with colored tights, shoes, fun scarves, jewelry, and cardigans! Once you get comfy with your core look, you'll be able to jump into a cute outfit just as fast as you used to pull on your favorite dress.

In chapter 9, we'll talk about my personal favorite core style for nursing—the tunic!

For Hopeful and First-Time Mommies: Make a pin board specific to maternity styles (just be aware, your friends and followers will probably view this as an announcement!). Get a solid idea of the color scheme you want to build from during this season (refer to Chapter 4!).

For Returning Champions: Sort your existing maternity wardrobe with your newly revised personal style and color scheme in mind. Give away the pieces that made you nauseated when you wore them last. If that's most of your wardrobe, then start buying cute maternity styles whenever you find a piece you like at a good price!

The Art of Layering
{Textures, Contrast, and Balance}

I got a pair of jeggings last month.

You know, those so-called "pants" that require a knock-down-drag-out fight to get on, and make you contemplate scissors when you have to peel them off? Yeah, those.

(I'd been in the market for a pair of dark-wash skinnies for months, and there they were, hanging way longer than the rest of the pants in the little rack in my favorite tiny thrift store, just my size and just $1.50! It was, as my mother would say, a jack-pot day at the thrift store. Oh, yes.)

Now, in case you're suddenly wondering if you should be taking fashion advice from a woman who is obviously confused about what is appropriate attire for a 30+ year-old body that has birthed three children, I assure you: I never wear these babies by themselves. Oh, no. That would be disturbing.

But these jeggings (jean-leggings) and other skinny-style pants in my closet are an essential ingredient to proper layering and balance in my mamma wardrobe. You never see much of these pants above my knee because I'm always wearing them under tunics—and it's what makes the outfit!

I believe that drape, flow, and layering are great strategies for flattering the child-bearing body, but first we need to learn the art of balance.

The basic idea is that an outfit should not entirely consist of all of one kind of fit or texture or weight of fabric. You should not have too much of one element in your ensemble. Wearing loose, shapeless pieces from top to bottom is no more pleasing to the eye than skin-tight, straining seams from neck to ankle. You must have some of both.

The looser the top (think tunic, drapey blouse, linen or gathered fabric), the more fitted you should go on the bottom. And if your pants or skirt are flowy or billowy, definitely pair them with a fitted top.

Here's another example, this time with fabrics. You have a favorite denim jacket and great jeans. Trying out the denim shirt look with this outfit is going to be overkill—totally out of balance. Instead, think what is in high contrast to denim—lace? Light-weight, drapey fabric? Knits? *Exactly*. Choose your top to contrast—not match—the rest of your ensemble.

Still wanna try rocking the denim shirt? Pair it with a long, flowy maxi skirt, or pants that are any material but denim.

Another area in which one can achieve contrast is with colors, although this one is very subject to personal preference. Choosing high contrasting colors in an outfit creates a bold look that may not match your personality. Still, be aware of each item you add to an outfit—does it bring a balancing level of contrast, or does it overwhelm the outfit in one direction? Having every item in your ensemble a particular shade of pink is going to be more Pepto-Bismol than peppy. Throw in some variation in shade, texture, or even a completely different color to make an outfit pop.

It's like a teeter-totter. On one side, you have light, frilly, weightless, airy elements of an outfit. On the other side are your denim, your leather, and your metal. A well balanced outfit has some of both, and isn't dominated by one or the other.

Don't save your leather boots for only your more rugged, masculine-inspired outfits—pair them with lace and frills. This is what makes an outfit memorable—when it is a combined melody of low and high notes.

"If you can get a sheer/silky button-up blouse to wear under a cardigan or jacket it creates beautiful diversity. The more varying texture or fabric you have in your wardrobe the better."
–Christa Taylor[3]

Now, if a sheer or shimmery shirt just seems too fragile for the line of work you're in—I totally get that. Save that silk blouse for a night out. But you can still apply the principle of balance to your casual, every day mommy outfit and feel the difference each time you glance in the mirror.

I have this big, brown sweater with a cowl neck I like to wear on chilly winter days here in Upstate NY. I pull it on and I feel all cozy and "right." But I've learned that it's important to pair that with the right thing on my bottom half or the good feeling goes away. A brown pair of loose-fit corduroys? I'm gonna feel like a bear in hibernation! But a pair of dark wash, slim fit jeans or a knee-length skirt with purple leggings? This brings balance to the outfit and I'm rocking the cozy-chic look as I do laundry or bake bread.

There was a time (a sad, sorry time) in which most of my wardrobe consisted of cotton knits and denim. I have nothing against denim, and it seems to be all the rage lately, but it is not a celebratory fabric for me. I'm in a season of life worth celebrating—let's have a little pizzazz, please.

Find an item in your wardrobe that stands out either by its fit or texture of fabric. Maybe it's a fuzzy, bulky sweater, or a bit of sparkle on a blouse. Experiment with balance by finding a second piece that is in high contrast to the first. See if you can figure out a way to wear them together. Discover that your wardrobe has more pizzazz than you thought by learning the art of balance and contrast.

Share the outfit you create with the hashtag #MomsEmbracingBeauty

Flexible Fashion
*{Tunics and Other Styles Your
Ever-changing Figure Will Love}*

A key to embracing our shape and style as mothers is letting go of a certain style that just almost never works for us. The look I'm talking about is well-tailored pants that fit like a glove (perfectly pressed and just the right length, mind you) and a blouse or shirt that hugs every curve just right and leaves no room for the imagination. The problem with this skin-tight silhouette is that as mothers, we rarely have our bodies in the "perfect" shape this style requires. We may breast feed, eat a balanced diet, and work out for months to lose that baby weight, and the week we finally get the jiggle under control, we find out we're pregnant again. Not only is it frustrating to attempt to fit our body into this look, it's not kind to the clothes budget to buy items and go for a certain look that *only* works for when we aren't carrying a single extra pound.

I'm advocating that we as mothers begin to embrace styles that allow for the fluctuation in weight and measurements that is a very natural part of this season. I think our problem is that we only allow ourselves to wear clothes designed for a changing figure when we're pregnant, and the rest of the time we expect our bodies to fit into clothes that leave no room for the flex of motherhood. The reality is, the months—or even years—leading up to a successful pregnancy and the years immediately following contain just as much flux in weight and shape as the nine months of pregnancy.

Friends who have struggled with infertility tell me that their weight often see-saws drastically on the path toward conception. And if you choose to breastfeed for a year or two, you have another's nutritional needs affecting your own metabolism and weight gain just as much as it did in pregnancy.

Yet we've succumbed to the idea that only in pregnancy can a woman embrace her shape and clothe it with styles that leave room for change. I tell you that we should ditch the styles that don't allow you to gain three pounds without busting a seam, or lose five pounds without having to take in that same seam.

Take jeans, for instance. I think we ask too much of our jeans. First of all, we want them to be the right wash, the right cut, and the right length for our legs, and then we ask them to cover our hips, butt, *and* waist with just the right support and fit. We're asking one article of clothing to cover over half our body—and the most changeable half, at that!

So many women are frustrated in the search for the perfect pair of jeans, and come to resent their bodies because they just don't *fit* the manufacturer's styling. Once they do find the perfect pair, and purchase them at the cost of a half a year's clothing budget, they must guard that precious asset with their life, fearing spills or stains, and ruing the day when a five pound weight change—whether up or down—dethrones their precious jeans and starts the frustrating quest all over again.

Those curves, pounds, and weight fluctuations—those are the natural and normal result of motherhood. Nothing to be ashamed of, and we shouldn't hate them for the sake of a certain pair of pants. Instead, I propose we find styles that gracefully clothe our curves while allowing for our constantly changing shape.

I'd like to quit hating my mother body, wouldn't you? Then it's time to embrace flexible fashion.

I confess, I saw this book as a chance to write as much on the subject of tunics as I wanted with no one stopping me. Tunics have changed my life. I went from never fitting my clothes right, to always feeling the right size.

6 Great Reasons to Love Tunics

1. A tunic is never boring. Whether it's a statement piece with lots of personality, or a simple, cotton shift, the drape of a tunic adds a measure of class and mystery to any ensemble. There's something about *not* hugging every curve that is feminine and graceful.

2. A tunic fits every figure. Tall and bony, short and round...Tunics work for all body styles. Why? Because tunics come in all different styles! I guarantee you there's a tunic that works for you (more on choosing your tunic style further on).

3. A tunic accents your strong points. It usually fits well over and thus accents your breasts (which are the one thing to write home about during motherhood, right?), and it stops right above the best part of your legs, highlighting the one part of our bodies that is still longer than it is wide. What's not to love?

4. Tunics cover a multitude of fitting issues. Pants too tight? Tunics cover that. Waist too loose? Tunics cover that. Belly trying to announce you're preggo when you're not? Tunics drape that bulge discreetly and draw attention elsewhere.

5. Tunics are good for the budget. A good tunic will carry you well into your first trimester and be there through nursing and beyond.

6. Tunics are a breastfeeding mom's best friend. They have plenty of room for boobs and babies and can often double as a nursing cover. Also? A tunic is one more layer between leaky boobs and embarrassment.

So, now that we've established that tunics are a style for mothers to embrace, let's talk about how to wear them and choosing the right style for your body type.

First, we need to see the tunic for what it is: a layer. I'm not a proponent of wearing tunic-length pieces as you would a dress, with little or nothing on your nether regions. Worn alone, tunics can be like a neon sign blinking all too brightly, instead of a discreet way of flattering what you've got going on. As we talked in the chapter on balance, if we have something flowy or loose on top, we let the bottom half be more form-fitting—and I don't mean bare legs! For a tasteful outfit, we're gonna want to have a little more between our legs and the world. Also, because of their looser styling, most tunics need a tank underneath—or, in winter, a sleeved shirt. So, as you shop for tunics, keep an eye out for the layers that you will pair them with: leggings or skinny jeans, and fitted tanks or shirts. Tunics are not meant to work alone.

Next, we need to think length. Generally, the taller you are, the longer tunic you're gonna need. And if you're petite, you can actually get the tunic look with something that's not even sold as a tunic. You're looking for that top to skim over your bottom and end somewhere between your crotch and your lower thigh. Any shorter and it's not going to do any good for disguising that ever-changing middle—in fact, a shirt that ends right at the fullest part of your hips or rear is actually going to draw attention to that area and make it look bigger—heaven forbid! Conversely, if you get too much length going on with your tunic, you're gonna look like you forgot to take your jeans off when you when you put on that "dress." If it looks like a dress, it's too long. If it highlights your heinie, it's too short. Got it?

Finally, we look at fit. I feel that the more ample a season I'm in, the more flow and drape I'm gonna need on top. The more you have to clothe, the lighter and drapier you want the fabric to be. Choosing a gathered and structured peasant blouse-style tunic when you've got a lot on top is only going give the illusion that there's more of you. But a knit or linen shift that "drips" off the curve of your breasts and flows toward your knees is going to draw smooth, long lines, giving a slimmer impression.

My favorite tunic-style tops lately have been the rayon, spaghetti strap-style sundresses that have been popular for a few years. With my height they actually fall just below my crotch. I wear them in summer with just a tank and shorts underneath, or through fall and winter with skinny jeans under, and a favorite cardigan and scarf layered over. They are incredibly versatile for changing sizes and seasons.

Although the tunic is the prima donna of flexible fashion, there are other styles we can find freedom in:

The Sweater Dress. As long as you don't mind the way this style tends to hug your curves, the sweater dress is just like the tunic in that it loves you through at least several inches of change, and allows for lots of fun layering and accessorizing.

The Wrap Dress. The few one-piece dresses I do have in my closet that have gotten decent screen time in the past 6 years have been wrap-style dresses. The wrap dress rocks because you've usually got several inches of play in the waistline allowing it to love you through more than just one waist measurement. And while it's at it, the wrap dress can be quite flattering, it's v-neck and fitted styling accenting whatever waist you've got that month. I've also had pretty good luck nursing in wrap dresses, if I layer a tank underneath them.

Long Cardigans and Jackets. Length in your layers is always a slimming strategy. Drawing vertical lines with your clothes lengthens your figure and lets your eyes ride right over those thick spots. A cardigan that shoots right past the waist and beyond the hips minimizes curves and extra pounds and is a great layer over a top or pants that aren't flattering you that month. I especially love them in black, which is a color that loves and forgives whatever shape my hips are in.

Maxi Skirts. Two words: Elastic Waist. Two more words: Long and slimming. Oh, and did I mention comfortable *and* sexy? The longer a visual line you can draw in your outfit, the slimmer you look. Waist to floor in a drapey fabric is flattering for any figure. Maxi skirts are my new love because they make me feel absolutely elegant *and* I don't have to give them up in pregnancy. I just wear them a little lower on my "waist." Plus, you don't have to shave your legs. Or find matching socks. Have I convinced you?

Jeans of all Sizes: When you grow out of favorite pair of jeans, don't cry. Chances are you'll see them again if you're willing to store them for a year! I stock jeans in sizes from 6 to 14, so that whatever size I am that month, I have a favorite pair that fit. Weight fluctuation is less of a hassle if you can dip into your closet for a size that fits rather than having to go shopping *again*.

Yoga pants are no longer the only option for you, mamma! Even when your jeans don't fit just right, you can cover the gaps or bulges with a tunic or another layer and quit stressing about your waist. Practice the art of finding and rocking flexible fashion and you'll spend fewer moments hating your size and more time loving the season of motherhood you're in.

Check out my tunic pin board on Pinterest and see if there are some styles that appeal to you. I've pinned lots of different body styles so you'll have plenty to choose from. Start your own pin board with styles that feature flexibility, such as the tunic, sweater dresses, wrap dresses, and long layers. Begin keeping an eye out and gearing your wardrobe toward articles that allow for flex in your waistline.

Celebrate finding the flexible fashion solution that works for you by sharing a photo with the hashtag #MomsEmbracingBeauty

Adding Personality
{Choosing and Rocking Those Accessories}

"The Lord wraps himself in light, as with a garment."
Psalm 104:2 NIV

This verse tells me that even God gets dressed, and He uses stars for His accessories! Way to go, God!

Most mammas I know wear jeans and T-shirts and there's nothing wrong with that. It works great for our active lifestyle. But putting accessories over or around those basic pieces is what transforms our ordinary mom-uniform into a look that's functional *and* stylish. Accessories are the way we personalize our look and define ourselves outwardly. Remember, what we wear is a song we sing to those around us. Is your song smooth and deep? Light and playful? Go back to your style board and listen for the music.

Most of us have tons of accessories lying around, but only a few we wear often. That's okay. All those castoffs are a sign that you have made progress on your journey. You know what doesn't work for you...have you found what does?

If accessories are new to you, take a deep breath, and understand they are not that complicated. For one thing, there are not normally fitting issues with accessories—it's not like trying to find a pair of jeans. Most scarves and jewelry are one-size-fits-all. Second, accessories are usually cheaper than the average article of clothing—unless you're talking designer purses, which, ahem, *I am not*. Experimenting and even making a few "mistakes" in your journey to find what's right for you doesn't have to have a significant impact on your wallet. And if those beads aren't your color, or the hat wasn't made for your brow, accessories are great at getting passed on to a friend and finding a new home.

Your guide for choosing accessories should be not just what's in style, but what's *you*. It's tempting to stock up on the latest trends but this can lead to piles of unworn necklaces and boxes of forgotten shoes. You should purchase items that thrill you, that you can see yourself wearing five years down the road, even if no one else is.

That being said, trendy accessories are a great way to keep your basic look up-to-date without spending a ton of money every time styles change. Audrey Hepburn's son, Sean, said, "My mother believed that a woman should find a look that works for her and use fashion and its seasonal changes to accessorize it, rather than be a slave to fashion, recreating one's look over and over again."[11]

Those who know their own style are not slaves to fashion fads because they wear what they love with confidence. So, let's explore how we can confidently accessorize!

Scarves

Although scarves have certainly become Über-popular lately, they are a classic that will always be in style for those who know how to wear them. So, taking the time to add a few different ties to your repertoire is a wise investment in your fashion future. One of my pet peeves is seeing people purposing to wear scarves because everyone else is, but having no idea how to tie them. Take that scarf up a notch and try these ties:

The Woven Noose

One of the most popular scarf ties is when one doubles their longish scarf in half, wraps the doubled length around their neck, and slides the ends through the loop. Quick and easy, but I find it gives me the appearance of a third boob. So a friend taught me this little trick to make the "knot" flatter and more flattering: Wrap the doubled length of your scarf around your neck, as described above, but only put one end of the scarf through the loop. Next, grab the loop and twist the lower half of it. Then weave the second end through the new loop you've created. Pull and fluff till it looks tidy (or messy—whichever you prefer!)

There! We've solved the third-boob problem! Be aware— when you wear your scarf in this awesome woven knot, complete strangers will come up and beg you to reveal your secret. Be sweet and oblige them. If you need to "see" it to get it, watch a video of me doing this tie here[12].

The Collar Tie

It's important that, along with a variety of scarves, you have a variety of ties to maximize each scarf's potential and complement different outfits. Many ties simply involve draping the scarf, necklace-style, from your neck, but this one spreads the bulk of the scarf around your collar and shoulders, providing a dressier look that works with lots of necklines.

Take opposite corners of a large, square or rectangular, scarf. Pass them around your neck, crossing in the back and bringing the ends to the front. Tie corners off in a double not. I like to twist the whole thing to the left and use the knot to accent one side of my collar. But you can also twist the scarf all the way around and hide that knot under folds at the back of your neck. If your scarf is really long, you will have to wrap it twice, or even three times around your neck. Experiment with what works for you and your scarf, and check out this video[13] to see my variations.

There are TONS of different scarf ties and how-to videos online; you can find your own favorite ties by checking out my Pinterest board "The Art of the Scarf."

Jewelry

Necklaces, earrings, bracelets, and rings—there are so many possibilities and styles! Here are some hints for wading your way through the overwhelming amount of choices in the jewelry department:

Zones and Balance

Jewelry is generally worn in 4 different zones: neck, ears, wrist, and fingers. Most of us have a favorite zone—that area that we love to enhance the most, and feel the most comfortable or excited experimenting with. My favorite is rings. Maybe yours is earrings. Knowing this is the zone in which you like to have the most variety when you get dressed helps you focus your search for the right pieces.

Don't overdo those zones. When donning your jewelry, it is not necessary to choose a piece for each zone. In fact, it is advised that one not wear jewelry in more than 3 of the 4 zones. (i.e., If you're wearing necklace and earrings, and rings beyond a wedding band, it's probably overkill to add 3 of your favorite bracelets!) But, as my sister likes to remind me, "Fashion rules were meant to be broken!" If jewelry in every zone is part of your unique look, then go for it!

Those who wear glasses have a 5th zone to work with, and it's important to make sure that the jewelry you put near your face doesn't clash or compete too loudly with your eyewear.

My friend, Natasha[14], has a great handle on the idea of balance and zones when adding jewelry to an outfit:

"If I'm wearing my glasses, I don't wear any jewelry. My face can't handle that much going on. I might throw on a scarf.

"If I'm wearing contacts and jeans, I put on dangly earrings. I often throw very glitzy earrings on if I'm wearing a hoody, just to have that added feminine pizzazz.

"If I'm wearing a skirt, I often try to find 'quiet' earrings that add dimension to my outfit but let the outfit be the center piece."

When I wear my glasses, I usually skip or go really small with earrings (pearls or cubic zirconia posts) and instead choose a strong beaded or textured necklace to balance out my frames.

Don't think that just because you wear glasses, or don't have your ears pierced, or can't stand to wear something around your neck that you can't wear jewelry. You will find your style if you're willing to experiment.

Choosing Material and Styles.

If you haven't already, you need to decide if you prefer silver or gold. A recent trend is to wear them together, but usually one tone or the other compliments your skin better, so it's wise to choose one and keep to it with most of your jewelry purchases. The simplest way to figure out which metal works for you is to hold a well-polished piece of gold or silver jewelry next to your face and see which stands out more. If your coloring tends toward cooler shades, the silver will compliment you well; gold usually stands out more with warmer skin tones. If you're still confused, I suggest you do what I did: ask your mom or another older woman who is blood related to you—she'll have similar skin tone and will probably have figured this out already.

But jewelry is no longer mainly made of fine metal—there's been a surge of all kinds of materials in jewelry, from felt to silk, paper to clay, and all those beautiful resin beads. Jewelry is the place to go wild with color, because it's a small part of your over-all look. It's totally okay if your jewelry doesn't come from a diamond retailer or cost you an arm and a leg. Each person has her own style and there's no rule that you have to love sparkle and diamonds! I find great delight (and a fair amount of stress reduction) in choosing necklaces and styles that are cheaper and more casual for my mommy-look. I prefer a cheap string of resin beads over a strand of pearls —first because it matches my every day style, and second, because I won't have to weep if a pudgy hand yanks it off my neck.

Your facial features can guide you when choosing jewelry. If you have thin lips, lighter coloring, and otherwise fine features, smaller, finer jewelry will compliment your face, and big jewelry may overwhelm your features. If you have wider lips, darker eyes and eyebrows and other bolder features, bigger, bold necklaces and earrings will work great for you. But remember, this is not a rule, but a guideline. Use it if it helps you learn what you love.

Mommy-Friendly Styles

I know a lot of moms, including myself, who are challenged to wear much jewelry especially in the season of nursing. Those idle baby hands can wreak havoc on ear lobes and necklace strands, and a diamond ring can too easily scratch a fat baby thigh during diaper changes. But we must not give up in adding personal touches to our look—we should be infusing the every-day with beauty and fun.

When I'm nursing, I replace necklaces with scarves, so I still have something around my neck but it's not breakable. I also have fun with rings with smooth-polished stones and, my personal favorite for when my babies are little—bracelets. Easy to slip on and low profile, bracelets are a great mommy piece. Wear several at a time, and you've got what's called an Arm Party!

You're Invited to an Arm Party!

Arm parties are all the rage now and I think they're a great style for moms. If you search Instagram for #armparty you can see people having all kinds of fun with different collections of bracelets. The thing to love about arm parties is there are no rules. Some are studies in diversity, others a statement of unity and belonging.

My arm party is actually more like an intimate gathering of a few close friends, comprised of three handcrafted silver bangles, sentimental gifts from my mother and aunt, who both have their own large collection of bangles. (There's actually some stiff completion going on between my mom and her sisters as they add bangles to their personal collections. I think the current winner is in the lead with 16!) The sound of my mother's bangles jingling together as she came down the hall to tuck me into bed is one of the most beautiful memories of my childhood.

Alone, a single bracelet doesn't sing very loud, but there is strength in numbers. When worn in multiples, bracelets can create a visual and audible chorus that becomes the focal point of an entire outfit. Bracelets are often cheap and unique ones like to hang out at thrift stores quite often. Begin collecting some favorites so you can try this mommy-friendly style.

Avoiding Competition

One final guideline: if you choose a bold, statement piece for one zone, it balances things out to have smaller, "quieter" pieces in the other zones so you're not competing. To make sure you have the pieces to back up a bold necklace or earrings, I recommend you have these basics:

- One smaller, pendant-style necklace. This one should be in your metal of choice and a simple style that works with most of your wardrobe.
- One pair of small, stud-style earrings that doesn't clash or compete with your basic necklace.

You can branch out with all kinds of statement necklaces, earrings, and bracelets beyond this, but having these basics will allow you to wear jewelry in several zones without looking like a display case. If you're afraid you're overdoing it, take this advice from Coco Chanel—"When accessorizing, always take off the last thing you put on."

Purses

The sheer amount and crucial necessity of stuff us mammas must haul around often has us resorting to the most utilitarian choices in the handbag department. But I'm gonna remind you that that purse will go with you everywhere and work really hard—kind of like a good bra—except this will be visible! So please, please make the effort to find a great purse or diaper bag so that your purse adds to your ensemble instead of dragging you down.

There are some great new diaper bag styles available to our generation that actually masquerade as designer bags. We really have no excuse for our bag to be frumpy. May I also remind you that a large, stylish handbag can double as a diaper bag? Think outside the box and be willing to make a statement with this standard element your wardrobe.

Bringing to mind what we learned about balancing textures, your purse is a great place to add a texture you don't usually wear. I'm talking about leather and sparkles and metal and pizzazz! Your personal color scheme should also be a deciding factor, ensuring that the color you choose will compliment most of your outfits, saving you from having to dump purse contents from one to another each time you go out.

I used to use canvas totes for everything, making my "purse" the frumpiest part of my outfit. This was really a problem when I actually went somewhere fancy. Finally, I found a great, navy blue leather purse at the thrift store. It complimented my personal color scheme, and looked as good with my Sunday best as my jeans. It held everything I needed, the leather was as sturdy as a tote, and it brought my errand-running uniform of jeans and T-shirt up a whole notch in the style department. I'm converted and have vowed to never let my purse drag down my style again.

Shoes

For those of you with normal-sized feet (says the poor gal with size 12 flippers) shoes are another great place to bring fun colors and textures to your wardrobe. Just be sure you have the basics before buying those neon green stilettos that will only go with one thing in your closet! I recommend:

- For Winter: One pair each dress shoes and boots in darker tones that match your personal neutral.
- For Summer: One pair each dress shoes and sandals that compliment your personal color scheme.
- For Casual: tennis shoes or sports sandals, or whatever footwear you like for going to the park.

Remember that even when choosing a pair of tennis shoes you can be mindful of your favorite colors and choose a style that will make you smile when you put them on. After the basics, feel free to branch out and use shoes to add pizzazz to any outfit!

Belts

I neglected belts for way too long in my wardrobe! Nothing defines what waist we have like drawing a line around it! Let's take advantage of this great little accessory. Even when we're pregnant, we can belt a blouse or dress above the belly to bring texture and definition to an outfit.

Again, I recommend the basics before branching out into more statement belts. A brown and a black belt in the width you prefer is a great start. After that, have fun with sparkles, colors, extra-wide or extra-thin. Realize if the belt you choose features a lot of metal accents, it's gonna compete with your necklace or bracelets. Keep balance in mind, and if the belt makes a very strong statement, you can back off on the jewelry front.

Accessories add the finishing touch to an outfit, and joy to your day. Learn to not consider yourself fully dressed until you've added at least a little something on top of the basics that is an expression of your personality. But make sure those things actually fit your lifestyle. I love Natasha's[14] advice on this:

> *"Make your accessories work for you. I work on a farm; I'm not going to be wearing 'pretty' clothes most of the time. But when I throw on a pair of glitzy earrings with my work jeans and sweatshirt—I feel better. I also buy pink barn boots. That helps a lot too."*

Find links, resources, videos and more at
http://trinaholden.com/embracing-beauty/extras/

- Visit my Pinterest Scarf Inspiration board and practice one new scarf tie. Try printing off a few tutorial graphics and taping them to the inside of your closet door to keep you inspired.

- Visit my Belted Beauty board to be inspired at how you can add belts to your look. Check out all the different styles of belts and take note of which one you'd like to add to your collection before your next shopping trip.

- Sort your shoes and make sure you aren't lacking the basics you need for each season. If you're good to go, plan your next shoe purchase to be something with a bit more personality and try accessorizing with your shoes!

Final Touches

{A Brief Note on Quick Hair and Even Faster Makeup}

Hooray! You're dressed! But on your final glance in the mirror, you do a double take. Unless you want the conversation to once again revolve around those dark circles under your eyes all the reasons you only got two hours of sleep last night, you're gonna have to do something—and quick.

Makeup

I'm a minimalist when it comes to makeup. My mother, a former Mary Kay consultant, taught me to apply classic colors in a way that accented my natural features without announcing loudly that I was wearing much of anything. Even as I've branched out beyond the classic lines she taught me, I have still stayed with natural tones and a bare minimum approach for two reasons:

1. If I'm gonna get out the door with any makeup at all, it needs to take me less than five minutes.

2. If I don't have time to get makeup on, I don't want my normal face to look vastly different than my made-up face.

That second point stems from a scarring experience I had as a child. I have a relative who wore bright blush, lipstick, fake eye-lashes—the whole nine yards—every day, no matter the occasion. Although she stayed with us for two weeks once, I only saw her one time without her makeup and it was scarring. She looked absolutely dead. From that day I vowed I would always wear my makeup in a way that simply enhanced my features, rather than painting over them completely.

Now, I'm not about to tell you how to do your face, but I am going to suggest that for a quick makeup routine that ensures your face doesn't scare people, start with the accent you can't spare and add more only if you have time.

May I Suggest the Layer Approach? (I know, I'm addicted to layering)

1. **The Rescue Layer.** This layer is whatever gets you out the door without looking dead. For most it's a bit of concealer on those dark circles, or a spot of blush, or it may be that lipstick is your quick rescue option.

2. **The Specialty Layer.** Here is where you zoom in on your favorite a zone—maybe it's lips, artfully-applied layers of concealer, or your eyes.

3. **The Party Layer.** This is the layer you add when you want to go all out. That layer of your face you only add when you have time or for special occasions.

Be realistic about how long you have to devote to your face, and give yourself grace to only wear the layer you have time for.

Here's my makeup routine, divided by layers

• Layer One—A quick all-over with a powder foundation. A dash of powdered blush to accent my cheek bones.

• Layer Two—My favorite zone to concentrate on is my

eyes. I draw eyeliner on my top lid, apply dark eye shadow on outside corner of the lid, and a lighter shade on inside corner.

- Layer Three—If I have another minute, I fill in the thin spots in my brows with a dark pencil. If it's evening, I'll add eyeliner to my bottom lid, and mascara to my lashes. If I'm really feeling like going all out, I'll add lipstick. But this is on very rare occasions, because as a mom of lots of cute babies and wife to a sexy man, I do a lot of kissing and lipstick gets in the way.

Hair

I have tried nearly everything with my hair since motherhood - short, long, layered, sculpted, curly, and straight. I have finally figured out that the best style for this season of my life is whatever is closest to my natural hair as possible. Here are my tips for mommy-friendly hair styles:

Find a hair stylist who will help find the best style for your hair type, not try and push a trendy cut on you just 'cause they wanna have fun with your hair.

Choose a wash-and-go style that has options for if you have time to spice it up. I love the wedge cut I had when Claire was younger, but it looked awful *unless* I had time to style it—which meant I only felt glamorous about once a week! It's much wiser to choose a style that looks cute Monday through Friday, than one that only looks good when you take extra time on weekends.

The longer your hair is, the more options you have. Let's face it - long hair is glamorous whether it's curly or straight, layered or even. Although long hair isn't an option for everyone, it is worth the patience it takes to grow it. Up-do's have more volume, and you make a statement just by doing nothing with it. So, try growing it out.

If short is your thing, why not go really short? A pixie cut, from what I've heard and seen from friends, can be a very mommy-friendly hairstyle because it dries so fast and styles so quickly. Just be sure you actually have time and money to get a trim every 4-6 weeks!

My sister reminds me that one's hair is the accessory you take everywhere (whether you like it or not!) so it's wise for us to figure out a style that works for us in this season.

A few styles I love that may work for your hair:

Scrunched Curls.

If you have any body in your hair at all, this may be a great style for you. How do you know if your hair will work for this style? If your hair is curly or wavy when it's wet, you have enough body to have fun with this style. Get a cut with layers that will make the most of your natural wave, then find a curl activator gel or spray. When you get out of the shower, towel dry your hair then spread your curl enhancer through it. Tip your head over and scrunch fistfuls of your hair toward your scalp to coax the curls to tighten. You can speed up the drying and enhance your curls further if you use a diffuser on your hair dryer for a few moments. But even without a blow drier, the right gel can help you retain the waves your hair gets when it's wet, and give you a wash and go look with some fun body.

Glam Bun and Sock Curls

If your hair is past shoulder length, you totally have to try this. Use an old sock to create a donut hair form by cutting off the toe and rolling it tightly on itself to create a donut shape. Put your hair in a high, top-of-your-head ponytail, secure with elastic, then flip your head over to insert the donut. Pull all the hair through the center, slide the donut down to the end of your hair, then start rolling the hair toward the outside, revolving the donut as you spread the hair all around evenly. Keep inverting the donut until it's tight to your scalp. Use bobby pins or mini claw clips to arrange hair to cover the sock or take care of loose wisps.

Wear bun as is, with red lipstick and big sunglasses, for a glamorous, retro look. Or, put the donut in before bed for full, gentle curls the next morning.

If you have had trouble getting the bun to work, you could purchase a manufactured hair form that's the same idea from a beauty supply store. They're inexpensive and made of netting so they help grip the hair better than the sock. You can also watch this video[15] of me installing my "donut."

Hair Sticks

Buns are so elegant, and can hide the need for a trim or the fact that you didn't have time to blow dry. I love to keep a quick bun in place with hair sticks, because they add interest and pizzazz. Plus, I find them gentler on my hair than elastics and bobby pins. It's easier to show than tell how to insert a hair stick, however, so visit this video[16] to see how I do it.

For more fun hair ideas, visit my Hairiness board on Pinterest.

Taking the time to study and streamline a makeup and hair routine that works for you not only makes you feel better as you face your day, but is a form of politeness. When our face is pleasing, it is a gift we can give the people around us. Finally, don't forget that a smile is an instant makeover. It transforms a face like no product or plucking can, because it's an expression of the heart.

• Sort your makeup drawer and put the stuff you use most often in a small makeup bag. You can keep the bag in the drawer, but transfer it to your purse if or when you're too busy to get makeup on before you leave the house. You can apply a layer or two in your rear-view mirror after the kids are safely buckled in their car seats before you pull out of the driveway, or go all out in the passenger seat if your husband is driving!

• Well-manicured eyebrows give your face a polished look even if you don't have time for makeup! Take two minutes to browse Pinterest for eye brow styles. (Check out my Eye Beauty board) When you find a style you think you like and could achieve with the brow hair God gave you, pluck away. If your kids see your tears and ask if it hurts, tell them "yes, but beauty is worth it." When you're finished, put your tweezers in your purse so you can maintain your look in the car next time you're in the passenger seat. If your brows are thin or blonde, consider finding an eyebrow pencil you can use to fill in and give your brows some sass.

• Prepare for those days when you don't have time to shower: Spend two minutes scrolling Pinterest for an up-do that works for your length of hair. Practice this several times when you don't have any pressure or anywhere to go. Keep the idea in the back of your mind (or with a photo on your phone!) for the next time you need cute hair in less time than it takes to shower.

• Create your own Hair Inspiration board on Pinterest and *only* pin styles that work for your hair right now. Use this board for last minute inspiration or when you have a few minutes to practice a new style.

The Art of Thrifting
{Building Your Wardrobe with Kids, on a Shoestring!}

If the idea of wearing someone else's cast off clothes gives you the heebie jeebbies, then this chapter is not for you. I'm not here to talk you into loving thrifting as much as I do, but…

- If you like treasure hunting
- If you like crazy awesome deals
- If you'd like to revamp your entire wardrobe for the price of a single article of new clothing

…then stick around! I'm going to teach you how to get the most out of your next shopping trip—even with kids in tow!

Thrifting is a part of my heritage. My mother has always bought the majority of her and her family's wardrobes at thrift and consignment shops. In addition to regular stops at thrift stores whenever we were out, we would also turn any visit from extended family into grand thrifting extravaganzas, aided by a grandparent's senior citizen discount, and funded by doting aunts and uncles. After retirement, my grandfather helped run his church's thrift store and though he is in his late 80's now, he still volunteers. Rather than disdaining second-hand clothing, my family celebrated thrifting as a sport and an art form.

When we lived on the homestead, we were so poor that the only place we could afford to shop was the Salvation Army—on half-off day. My mom went into town on Tuesdays with religious faithfulness to wash eight mega loads of farm-dirty clothes at the laundromat and to shop for a family of nine from whatever tags were half off at the tiny local Salvation Army. I remember many times when a run into town on another day of the week saw us dipping in for a little retail therapy, finding a treasure that wasn't on sale (yet), and tucking it stealthily in between the ugliest items on the rack, in hopes it would still be there next Tuesday. More often than not, it still was, and we rarely paid full price for anything. The only items I remember buying brand new in those years were boots and bras.

Following her lead, I now clothe my own family of five almost exclusively from the thrift store. Birthday gifts and hand-me-downs certainly give us a head start many seasons, but if I have a clear idea of what we need and am faithful to visit the thrift store with a good plan, we can usually avoid expensive trips to the mall.

I especially love the thrift store for building my own wardrobe because I have found there is wider scope for the imagination and a much broader opportunity for individuality than shopping at a store that only serves up one brand, style, and season of clothing at a time. Where else can you find skinny jeans and a vintage muumuu (that might make a great maxi skirt) under the same roof? Show me another store that boasts name brand linens, housewares, couches, *and* infant clothes at deep discounts every Thursday! The thrift store is the place for me.

But then came kids. You all know what I'm talking about. Grocery shopping is hard enough with kids in tow, and there you find everything you need in the exact spot it was last time! But when clothes shopping, you must search for the right size and style, and then you have to try it on! And thrift stores—oh my! The hunt is even more involved, the environment can be dirtier, and the time it takes to find and make decisions on your purchase can be doubled. Can we really do this thing with kids in tow?

The only reason I can say "yes" is because I've done it, and I know lots of woman who do as well. Here is where I'm going to share a cart-full of strategies you can try to help you toward more successful thrifting adventures as a mommy.

Make a Plan

Going into the thrift store without a plan is no way to save money. If you buy everything that's a "good deal" you'll return home with a pile of items that won't come together into any ensemble, and a wallet that won't support your going back to remedy the situation.

Our first step then, to a successful thrifting excursion, is to know our personal style and have a color scheme in mind. If you haven't done so yet, follow the suggestions in chapters 4 and 5 to get a solid idea of colors and styles you are looking for.

Next, make a list of the top items you need right now. This list will help you prioritize your time and money as you find and choose items. I usually keep such a running list of items I need to watch for in my home management binder or a slip of paper I keep in my wallet. On a given month, my list might look like this:

1. Shoes for Jesse
2. Skinny black belt for me
3. Clip on earrings for craft project
4. Church clothes for Claire
5. Tunics (tunics are perpetually on my list!)

When the list gets long or a need gets urgent, it's time to go!

But you must plan your shopping on the right day. Most thrift stores are open six days a week, but many stores have regular sales days. For example, the Salvation Army chain of thrift stores uses colored tags to price their clothing, and a different colored tag will be discounted (usually by 50%) on different days, with one day being "Family Day" offering a whopping four colors on sale. That is the day to go! Call ahead and find out which days are going to offer the best deals on the items you're looking for—there are often sale days for shoes, furniture, and linens, as well.

Shopping with Kids

List made, day chosen, now you must initiate Operation: Shopping with Kids. You cannot expect to have a successful trip without adequate preparation and strategizing.

Tips for thrifting with kids

Make the thrift store one of your first stops, while the kids are still fresh. If your thrift store doesn't offer a public bathroom, make a pit stop somewhere else before you begin shopping.

Have a well-packed purse, including snacks for kids, diapers for babies, wipes for cleaning little hands, and water bottles for all.

Bring a friend. Bribe her with lunch (either out-and-about or some homemade yumminess when you get home). She can help watch the kids while you try things on.

If you don't have a friend crazy enough, here's what you do: put all children small enough directly into the cart. It's no longer for merchandise, it's a mobile playpen (you can hang your clothes around the outside edges). Give the babes a snack and get going. When they get antsy, wheel your party over to the book section, find them each one of those obnoxious musical books, and head out again.

Be sensitive to your kids' needs and attention spans. If you quit before you've found the perfect pair of jeans, but while everyone's still happy, it will remain a positive experience in their minds and you can try again next week without a revolt.

Dressing rooms—grab a toy or book for each child and get a dressing room you can wheel the whole cart into if you have that option. Just train your boys to turn their backs while the ladies dress.

Involve your children in the decision making—ask their opinions, engage them in conversation while you shop. Teach them to enjoy the process by letting them be a part of the hunt for the perfect item.

You're in the store with a cart full of kids—where do you start?

The Zone Strategy

I like to shop the store by zones, and I choose which zones to hit first based on which items are higher priorities. I look at my list and remember my son needs shoes, and that if I don't find a pair soon, we're gonna have to spend the money for brand new ones (which he may grow out of in three months). So I head to the shoe section first and spend as long as it takes to thoroughly comb the selection and find a pair that will work.

Next I wheel my cart and kids over to the belt rack and see if there's a nice, skinny black belt to complete the outfit I'm trying to copy from my Pinterest board.

I work my way from zone to zone in order of priority, rather than store layout. I just can't afford the luxury of browsing the entire store row by row for any and all treasures that may fit my fancy. That kind of shopping is reserved for when I'm alone, or my husband has time off to come with me (he loves thrift shopping, too, being raised by a woman who's thrifting abilities rival my own mother's). If I have to leave without covering the whole store, or finding everything on my list, that's okay. It's not the thrift store's fault—the same thing could happen at the mall.

You could spend three hours in the thrift store every time you go, but I suggest shorter trips. Let yourself go to the thrift store just to look for jeans. Or just for dress clothes for your kids. Or just for layers to bring your wardrobe into the next season. Even though thrift stores offer the potential of a one-stop-shop for the whole family, you often need to specialize, thinking of the thrift store as just a shoe store on some days, or simply a kids' clothing store on others. If you want to make thrifting a family practice, you need to make it as positive as possible, and a big part of that is not wearing your kids out on the quest.

Follow the Recipe

Another shopping strategy is to use a recipe. You saw a cute outfit on Pinterest and you want to recreate it. You've got about half the components you need already in your closet, but you're missing a couple specific items. Print the inspiration photo so you have your "recipe" with you, or pull up the photo on your smart phone.

As you search each aisle, look for anything that remotely fits the description of what you're looking for. If it holds any possibility, throw it in the cart. I try to bring a lot into the dressing room, because I find 20% is a high rate of success when finding out if an item on the rack actually fits and works for the look I'm going for.

When filling a recipe, you need to be able to make substitutes. What's the most important aspect of the item you're looking for? Texture, shape, or color? Be willing to bend on one or the other if the finished look will still match the overall feel of your inspiration photo. Identify the key things you love about the outfit, and go for those.

Hidden Potential

Do you love the print of that dress but don't ever actually wear that style? Try up-cycling! Be open to the possibilities of turning an item into something else that's more your style. Because I'm so tall, it's hard for me to find skirts that actually hit my ankles and qualify as a maxi style, so I've made most of my longer skirts from big old jumpers or two-piece sets that I spent a few dollars on and an hour or two remaking. As a seamstress, I find the thrift store to be a great source for fabric, whether it be a set of curtains or sheets or a plus-sized skirt. Even if you're not an experienced seamstress, repurposing a garment is often as simple as a few straight seams, and it's a great place to begin to learn to sew for yourself because the cost and effort involved is significantly less than creating something from brand new materials. A few lessons in sewing basics from an aunt or friend can further broaden the possibilities of the thrift store for you and your family.

How Often Do You Need to Shop?

Not as often as you think. When you learn to purchase items that flex with your shape, and embrace the art of layering to move from one season to the next, your clothing needs will be fewer and shopping trips less frequent. When you buy things you love and that work for you, these items will be in your closet for years, requiring only occasional infusions of a few new items.

Kids are another thing, of course, because they like to grow out of their clothes, like, all the time. Here are some various routines that may work for you:

- Seasonally—I shop seasonally, meaning about the time I switch out my children's summer wardrobe for fall, or winter stuff for spring, I take stock and plan an hour at the thrift store along with my other weekly errands. Usually I'll attempt to hit one or two thrift stores per week for a few weeks until I've rounded out our wardrobe, and then I don't have to clothes shop again for several months.

- Weekly—If it fits into your routine, my mother's strategy of faithfully going once a week and purchasing anything we needed at the moment or in the foreseeable future is another strategy. This works if well if your thrift store is located along the route of your weekly grocery shopping or other trips to town.

- Monthly—You can go once a month, devoting the entire day to thrift store after thrift store, like my mother-in-law does. This makes a long day for kiddos, so definitely plan to bring that friend along to help, or leave the littlest kids with a babysitter so they can get their naps.

Finding the routine that gives you just the right amount of retail therapy and results that you need for you and your family, may take a while. Embrace the process of figuring out how to make the thrift store work for you and your family.

I would caution against going too frequently. Although I love me some good retail therapy as much as the next careworn mommy, the danger of thrift stores is that you can *always* find something to take home. Which means you will *always* be spending money. Even if it's just a few bucks at a time, it will add up if you don't exercise some self-control!

How to Avoid Buyer's Remorse.

Most thrift stores have a "no return policy." Although this may seem harsh and inconvenient, it really is a blessing in disguise. Knowing you must love your purchase or you've wasted your money will train you to choose wisely and not waste energy on items that don't work for your wardrobe. Yes, it forces you to be decisive when that may be the last muscle you want to exercise on your day out, but you will grow in this area through practice. Although I used to be very indecisive, and brought home many the wrong item from a shopping trip, I have learned to assess an item and to shove it back on the rack or into my cart very quickly by asking the right questions.

10 Questions to Ask to Avoid Bringing Home a Wardrobe Orphan:

1. Can I make an outfit with this item and what I have at home?

2. Can I make an outfit with this and something I have in my cart or can find in the store?

3. Does this item fit my personal color scheme? Or is it a strategic departure?

4. Does it fit me well, or do I have time this week to make the needed adjustments?

5. Is it trendy or classic? If trendy, am I willing to wear it even when others consider it out of style?

6. Am I buying it just because it's a name brand at a great price, or because I truly love it?

7. Am I buying it because others will think I'm stylish, or because I feel it is truly *my* style?

8. Will this item flex with me through more than one waistline measurement?

9. Will this item serve me well nursing or preggo, or only when I'm neither? (It better be cheap if it is the latter!)

10. Does this item have the potential to bring me joy when I wear it?

I don't bring home an item unless I can answer yes to at least several of these questions. Looking at an item in the light of my current wardrobe, my personal style, and the context of motherhood keeps me from buyer's remorse.

Building Your Child's Wardrobe from the Thrift Store

Many people express frustration at any attempt to find good kid's clothes at the thrift store. I agree that there's an awful lot of junk at thrift stores and kids clothes, especially, take such a beating it can be hard to find articles in good shape. But the fact that kids grow so fast means that there are like-new items out there, and you can find them if you're willing to make the effort. Here are my suggestions:

Have a Plan of Attack

Plan your trip well, and if your time is limited by other errands and your kid's stamina, devote your shopping time just to the kid's department, or even one kid's needs per trip.

Have a clear idea of what sizes and what type of clothing you already have and what you actually need. My current list includes pants for my two year old, but not shirts—for some reason the hand-me-down bin was shirt rich and pant poor. Don't waste your time sorting through items that aren't a high priority.

Choose a Color Scheme

I know this sounds idealistic—I mean, it's hard enough trying to find something that's the right size and in decent shape, adding a color scheme is just one more criteria to meet! But the same principles that you use for your own remorse-free purchases applies to your kid's clothes. If you buy everything you find that fits and is in good shape, you will end up with a ton of cheap clothes, but nothing will coordinate. You might as well just go spend the money to buy them brand new clothes unless you're willing to take the time to find mix and match items and create outfits as you search.

When Claire was a baby, I stuck to purple for clothing. When people asked about what to buy her for gifts, I said, "Her favorite color is purple!" and when I made clothing purchases, I stuck to that purple color scheme, ensuring that most everything she owned, from socks to Sunday dresses, coordinated.

She's four now, and likes a bit more variety in her wardrobe, but we still stick to certain colors when we purchase stuff because when I bring an odd item home like a pair of leggings or a sweater, I like to know that it will match or complete at least a few outfits. Her current color scheme is pinks and purples. This doesn't mean I don't buy the occasional blue or green shirt when shopping, but if I vary from our color scheme, I mentally check to see that the new shade at least coordinates with the majority of what we own.

Last fall, on top the weather changing, my six year old had a growth spurt. He suddenly needed everything in his wardrobe replaced. We headed to the thrift store with the goal of dress pants, jeans, dressy sweaters and shirts, and short and long-sleeved T-shirts he could work and play in. We combed the entire boy's clothing section and actually found a lot in his size. We narrowed down our purchases to a color scheme that included his favorite colors (red, navy blue, and grey), and I didn't choose a shirt unless it matched at least two pairs of pants, or a pair of pants unless several shirts coordinated with it. This all took some time as I wrangled with an impatient two year old, and kept losing Claire as she played hide and seek between the clothes, but we came home with five pairs of pants and eight shirts that gave us over a dozen different outfits, all for $18. That was certainly a jackpot day, but even if it had taken three different trips to accumulate his new fall wardrobe, it still would have been a significant savings over having to purchase all of that brand new!

Involve Your Kids in the Process

Another key to not bringing home purchases that don't end up getting worn is to let your kids help in the process. If they are old enough to get themselves dressed in the morning, they are old enough to be helpful in the process of building their wardrobe, and you're much less likely to get grief from them when it's time to get dressed if the options in their closet are things they helped choose at the store.

On our big fall shopping trip for Jesse, I found some great shirts in shades of orange. They looked good to me, so I put them in the cart. But when my boy expressed a decided dislike for anything orange, I put them back on the rack. No matter how high the quality or how low the price, it's not a deal if it's not going to be worn, same as when I'm shopping for myself.

My kids are young right now, and more of a hindrance than a help when I shop, but if I'm willing to train them today, there will come a day when we can take a "divide and conquer" approach at the thrift store, each child finding and choosing his or her own purchases, leaving me time to shop for myself!

Pray

There's no question that clothing our children frugally is a challenge. And there's nothing that's too small to bring to God—even a trip to the thrift store. Pray—out loud—for the success of your trip as you embark. Show your children you are depending on God as you attempt to fulfill your role as mother and homemaker. Pray specifically, so that you will have concrete examples of answered prayer to help build the faith of even your youngest child. Pray for grace to handle the challenges of managing your children in the store. Pray for obedient hearts and good attitudes from your kids. Pray that you can be a testimony to those around you as you shop. Remember that you are choosing the way of a wise woman, looking to the ways of your household, and attempting to clothe your family well (Proverbs 31:21 and 27) and the Lord can and will reward your diligence.

Thrift Store Experiments

- Search out a list of thrift stores within driving distance of you. Make some phone calls to find out which day would offer the best sales. Call a friend and plan a thrifting excursion for that day.

- Scan your Pinterest board for an outfit you'd really like to create for the next season. List its elements, check your closet for components, and then take your recipe to the thrift store. See if you can recreate the outfit entirely from what you have or can buy second-hand. Don't give up if your first trip isn't successful. Thrifting takes practice!

- If you've never taken your kids thrift shopping, make a solid plan, pack your diaper bag well, and head out. Keep your expectations low, and your eyes peeled for a deal. Make enjoying the process a higher goal than finding everything on your list. Celebrate every treasure found!

Ambassadors of Beauty
{A Commission}

"Mom, what are these bumps on your face?"

I'm distinctly aware in that moment that the tone of my voice when I answer her will inform and shape her understanding of beauty.

"They're wrinkles!"

"Oh!" She smiles at this new vocabulary word. Wrinkles must be something nice because mommy smiled when she said it. And when she smiled, there were more bumps on her cheeks and around her eyes. Wrinkles are interesting—lines that add punctuation and personality to a face.

My mother defined beauty for me. She began to grey when I was twelve, just at that age I was beginning to analyze and consciously define beauty for myself. One of the greatest gifts my mother gave me was not dyeing those grey hairs. My mother had always been beautiful to me, her child, and as we both matured, my definition of beauty grew to include silver grey highlights streaking the hair of the first woman I considered beautiful.

To this day I will claim my mother is the most beautiful woman I know. Some call this love's blindness. I declare that it is how our eyes are supposed to focus. If we look at things with love, we see people the way God does: exquisitely beautiful works of art.

It's time, sisters, to take the challenge—to take what we've learned and gird ourselves to make our countenance, our home, and our world a little more beautiful than it was yesterday. We are called to this because as humans we are God's crowning creation. He made earth, light, stars, cheetahs, orchids, oaks, and inchworms and said it was good. But by His own admittance, He was just warming up for when He made man and woman, and said, "This is very good!" because He'd made us in His image. And so began our commission here on earth to be ambassadors: of His love, His truth, and His beauty.

Beyond Permission

I used to think I needed permission to buy nice clothes, to take the time to do my hair, to put on makeup, to "feel" pretty. Permission didn't come often—only for the most special occasions did I feel it was okay. This misconception came from a devaluing of beauty in my mind. I did not realize that beauty—whether a pleasing outfit, a flower arrangement, or a melody—had such high value in God's eyes.

Meditating on the many facets of embracing beauty I've shared with you in this book has moved me beyond permission to dabble in pretty things, to a commission to be an ambassador of beauty to the world around me.

We are to define beauty for our children and teach them to celebrate it. Pointing out beauty in nature, praising their own attempts at identifying and creating beauty, and letting them see us intentionally embracing beauty will elevate beauty to its God-intended value in their eyes.

We are to accept God's definition of beauty and walk in it, with our head held high and a smile on our face. And when others notice us, it will be for the love that accents every angle—confidence in God's love for us and a selfless love for others because we are no longer consumed with the effort of bolstering our own worth with what we wear.

When we, as mothers, dress with confidence in a season when so many lose heart and give up, those watching will wonder, and when they see that our clothes coordinate with the joy in our hearts, they will surely wonder if we are royalty.

Let's dive into the joy He intended for us when He created beauty. Let's dress like daughters of the King!

Acknowledgments

If you've gotten the impression as you read this book that it was really a group effort, you'd be right. So many beautiful women gave so generously of their words and time to this book, and I feel humbled to have the privilege of walking this journey with them.

Rachel Hurd has taught me so much about embracing beauty and she totally rocks thrifted fashion. She also practically wrote an entire chapter for this book! Check out her blog if you want to read more from her (fashiongonethrifty.blogspot.com).

Shannon, Gretchen, and Amanda listened to my first ideas regarding this book, and their encouragement gave me the gumption to follow the call to write a book about beauty.

DeeDee generously contributed her expert advice on properly fitting bras, filling in an area I was weak in. Mandy, Diane, Ginger, Rachel and Jess graciously shared their experiences in this delicate area, helping me to laugh and enjoy the process.

Kristina, September, Diane, Kalyn, Traci, Natasha, Cynthia, Christin, Kateri, and Kris, and the rest of the my wonderful mastermind group prayed for me and cheered me on through the entire process. Never have I been more in need of the prayers of friends, and never has God shown me as clearly the beauty that is found in community than with this project.

Thanks to Lisa Jo for gracing my book with her benediction of a forward. Her support meant so much as I brought the book to completion.

And thank you to all my blog readers and friends online and offline, who answered my questions, prayed for me, provided quotes, and spurred me on by repeatedly reminding me of how much they were looking forward to my book. Deb W. Kelly A., Sara E., Stacey, Tiffany, Wendy, Claire P. Jennifer K., Lizzie B., Erin O., Jeannie P. Lisa, Jessica T., Rebekah H., and Jodi M.—thank you! Your encouragement meant so much!

Many thanks to my mother, who defined beauty for me and taught me the art of thrifting. And to my sisters Anja, Olivia, and Anneke, who have inspired me so much in the journey to embracing beauty. No one rocks personal style like my sisters!

Of course my husband, Jeremy, gets a huge thank you as he is a huge part of whatever I accomplish online or off! This man has elevated teamwork to an art form. I'm blessed by his enthusiastic support of my love for and call to write, and for the beautiful cover and format he created for this book. Oh, and for loving me and my body through every shape and season of motherhood.

And to God, who whispered the idea for this book, and then waited patiently for me to embrace the call with the joy He intended me to experience in the process. This book was all His idea, and He is truly the source of any truth or beauty my words reveal.

Notes

1 Amanda Medlin http://amandamedlin.com

2 Ginger Truitt http://gingertruitt.com

3 Christa Taylor http://www.empoweredtraditionalist.com

4 Rachel O'Neill http://purposefulwife.blogspot.com

5 Rachel Hurd http://fashiongonethrifty.blogspot.com

6 Beth Ricci http://redandhoney.com

7 Bamboobies http://ow.ly/jt8ik

8 Rebekah http://simplyrebekah.com

9 Nursing Cami http://ow.ly/jt8p6

10 Claire Printz http://www.lemonjellycake.com

11 *"Audrey Hepburn, An Elegant Spirit: A Son Remembers,*
   by Sean Hepburn Ferrer" http://ow.ly/jt8G2

12 Woven Noose http://youtu.be/iwHggPk-VBo

13 Collar Tie http://youtu.be/bxFWpkDuaf4

14 Natasha Metzler http://natashametzler.com

15 Glam Bun http://youtu.be/dt7KZArS9Xg

16 Hair Sticks http://youtu.be/M_0NLc5wHD4

You can also find these links and resources at
http://trinaholden.com/embracing-beauty/extras/

About the Author

Trina has gained a total of 130 pounds in pregnancy and has lost, ahem, not quite that much. But she's still smiling. You can find her wearing purple most days and learning to see her kids as inspirations, not interruptions, as she pursues her passions to write, encourage, eat real food, and embrace beauty.

Follow along on her latest adventures on
trinaholden.com

Also by Trina Holden:
Real {Fast} Food:
Plan Better, Cook Faster,
Eat Healthier
trinaholden.com/realfastfood

Say hello on Facebook, Twitter, or Instagram!

facebook.com/TrinaHoldenWrites

twitter.com/TrinaHolden

instagram.com/TrinaHolden

18635968R00067

Made in the USA
Charleston, SC
13 April 2013